A MAN SENT BY GOD
THE LIFE OF PATRIARCH
ATHENAGORAS OF CONSTANTINOPLE

A MAN SENT BY GOD
THE LIFE OF PATRIARCH
ATHENAGORAS OF CONSTANTINOPLE

Demetrios Tsakonas

Translated from the Greek
by
GEORGE ANGELOGLOU

HOLY CROSS
ORTHODOX PRESS
Brookline, Massachusetts

Reprint 2022

© 1977 Published by Holy Cross Orthodox Press

50 Goddard Avenue

Brookline, Massachusetts 02445

Library of Congress Cataloging in Publication Data

Tsakonas, Demetrios Gr

A man sent by God.

Translation of: Athenagoras ho Oikoumenikos ton neon ideon. Includes bibliographical references and index.

1. Athenagoras I, Ecumenical Patriarch of Constantinople, 1886-1972.

2. Patriarchs and patriarchate—Biography. I. Title.

BX395.A8T7613 281.9'092'4 [B] 77-77699

Library of Congress Catalog Card No. 77-77699,

Printed in the United States of America

Cover design by Nicholas J. Botsolis

ISBN 978-0-916586-07-2 (Paperback Edition)

To

Dr. C. N. Hadjipateras

In warm and devoted friendship which was nourished and devoped by
the inspiring personality of the great Patriarch.

Contents

CHAPTER 4

THE PHILOSOPHY OF ATHENAGORAS

CHAPTER 5

PHOTOGRAPHS

PUBLISHER'S NOTE

The Holy Cross Orthodox Press, housed at the Holy Cross Greek Orthodox School of Theology, is happy and proud to publish Demetrios Tsakonas' A Man Sent By God: The Life of Patriarch Athenagoras of Constantinople.

A man of peace, reconciliation, and love, Patriarch Athenagoras left an indelible mark wherever he served God's Holy Church. His contributions to the Church in the United States and in particular to Holy Cross School of Theology were of fundamental importance, as were the personal impressions he made on all to whom he spoke and embraced. His memory will truly be eternal among us.

Thanks are due to His Eminence Archbishop Iakovos for his encouragement and support, to Miss Terry Kokas of the Greek Archdiocese for her assistance in securing the photographs used in this volume, to Mrs. Sophia Caparisos for preparing the manuscript for the printers, and to Mr. Norman Themely for preparing the index and furnishing the idea for the cover.

N. M. Vaporis

ΩΩΩ

ECUMENICAL PATRIARCH
ATHENAGORAS
A MAN OF VISION AND RECONCILIATION
MARCH 25, 1887 — JULY 7, 1972
VASILIKON VASILEVOUSA

"COME AND LET US LOOK INTO ONE ANOTHER"

FOREWORD

To present a complete portrait of the Patriarch, [writes Father Maurice Villain,] one must have real genius—the pen of a George Bernanos, the paintbrush of a Territi, the chisel of a Michelangelo; and to portray the spiritual greatness of the Patriarch, one would even need the art of Rublev. The fact is that everything about Patriarch Athenagoras is larger than life. Why, the very mention of his name recalls to mind the great men like Abraham, Moses, and Melchisedec.

So, I am convinced that the portrait I was asked to draw is an impossible task. I cannot draw those huge eyes of his that remind you of a Byzantine icon; I cannot depict that wonderful great beard which exudes an aroma of balsam; I cannot describe his superb straight-backed figure, which moves with grandeur and poetry during a service. No, I shall have to limit myself to expressing one of his mannerisms only—his way of greeting you. When Patriarch Athenagoras greets you, you feel that his look envelops you with love and respect; his two great arms reach out and embrace you with warmth and humanity, you feel inspired to climb to the summit, where the prophet lives, towards the gospel of love and unity. And a convincing voice suddenly murmurs in your ear. "We have the same credo, the same Christ, the same saints, and the same martyrs. Whoever you may be, whether a lowly pilgrim or a well-known personality, you have been captivated."[1]

Patriarch Athenagoras, 268th Archbishop of Constantinople, was the first name on the list of the three hundred fifty bishops who today lead more than one hundred and fifty million Orthodox Christians. He occupied the sacred throne of the Greek Church that is situated in the historic Phanar district of (Constantinople) Istanbul. This is the very heart of the entire Orthodox Christendom.

The personality of Athenagoras has really three dimensions: the first is the greatness of his thinking, which blends perfectly with his great physical stature; the second dimension is his breadth of mind, which resembles in some way his gigantic embrace; and the third is his depth, which gradually becomes apparent as you come under the spell of the dynamic spiritual power of the Patriarch.

Athenagoras combines the individual characteristics of a leader of a nation, a Patriarch, and a prophet. In his forehead, you discern intelligence and creativeness. His eyes—which, as Christ said are the lamps of the body—mirror all his psycho-dynamic strength. They are superb brown, penetrating eyes; their look constantly probes, searches, questions, analyzes: yet at the same time, their look gives you encouragement and help and a sense of peace and fulfillment. His lips always utter gentle and courteous words, which are an extension of the inner man at peace with the world and whose capacity for love is endless. His language is a new language, the language of a pioneer leader. He dislikes pedantic monologue; he loves dialogue, as Jesus Christ our Lord did.

As soon as World War II ended, I met Athenagoras with a group of young intellectuals at the Greek Archdiocese of America in New York. The

1. Informations Catholiques Internationales, No. 320 (Jan. 15, 1969).

group included Dr. C.N. Hadjipateras, who had just published an important book on the Greek resistance of 1940-1945, Dr. E. Papaconstandinou,
and a lawyer named G. Lambropoulos. The Archbishop's vigorous and
warm personality immediately captivated me. Athenagoras was a strange
mixture of idealism and realism; he held you captive with his impressive
and dramatic speech, but also with his incisive logic, with which he would
afterward analyze current political, social, and intellectual events. Perhaps
he was the first Greek Orthodox leader of the older generation who went
abroad not to isolate himself, but in order to learn and understand the
problems of other countries. His enemies have called him a Protestant, a
Catholic, a Turkophile, a friend of the Americans and of the Russians, and
many other things. Strangely enough, all these accusations were dropped
only to be replaced by others equally contradictory.[2] There is only one true
fact Wearing the modest, black robes of the Orthodox priest, he lived in the
great city of New York listening and feeling the pulse of the United States
and of the world.

He was considered to be a liberal, modern, and up-to-date man;
yet he walked about in his long, black robes and peculiar clerical
hat—a sort of anachronism in the contemporary consumer society
of New York. But if you were to speak to him for a few minutes, you
would change your mind. He would win you over, whatever your
background, whatever your religious beliefs. "He knows how to pull
down the fences and put in their place the open space of love, understanding, and compassion. That body of his is activated by a strong
peaceful heart which seems to synchronize its pulse with the heartbeat
of humanity."[3]

2. A. G. Panotis, Paulos vi. Athenagoras A Eirenopoioi (Athens, 1971),
pp: 43-44.
3. D. Tsakonas, "Athenagoras A'," Threskeutike kai Christianike Egkyklopaideia I, 602-06.

In particular, he hated fanaticism and he was very conscious that despite his own biblical appearance, he lived in modern times and not in the Middle Ages. He was a real spiritual leader without any political ambitions whatsoever. For this reason, he disapproved of Archbishop Damaskinos when the latter became Regent and Prime Minister in 1944. Similarly, he did not see eye to eye with Archbishop Makarios. He considered that a spiritual leader was permanent, whereas a political leader was ephemeral. Yet Athenagoras, somehow, was both permanent and ephemeral, Orthodox and pan-Christian, Greek and international, without in any way betraying his American passport—when he was an American citizen—or his Turkish nationality since hesincerely believed in Graeco-Turkish friendship and unity. He was indeed, a great internationalist. The narrow parochialism and the religious fanaticism of the old Greek Orthodox emigrants to America were entirely foreign to him. For this reason, he was admired by all religious leaders of the West. At the same time, all Orthodox people living outside Greece, whatever their nationality, acknowledged him as their natural leader. Athenagoras did not seek this recognition; it was automatically bestowed upon him.

One should emphasize that Athenagoras was perhaps the only leader who knew and understood the logic of the West He was neither for nor against such logic, but he knew how to interpret this logic and how to deal with the various political repercussions.

Such, therefore, was the charismatic personality that listened to us in that impressive building of the Greek Orthodox Archdiocese of North and South America in New York. Athenagoras' eyes filled with concern when I gave him a frank analysis of Greece's difficult occupation years. I pointed out that teachers at that time had failed to join the resistance movement and that most politicians and intellectuals had been indifferent and apathetic to the struggle against the forces of occupation. Doubt showed in his eyes. "Why this nihilistic criticism?" asked the Archbishop. "Does that mean that everything in post-war Greece is worthless and that all leadership is bankrupt?" The Archbishop was actually questioning the success of a Communist uprising in Greece and the alternative of a socialist regime imposed by the army. In those days, the entire leadership of the nationalist forces (the King, Sophocles, C. Tsaldaris, and Papagos) was being challenged by the younger generation. This generation had done its duty during the difficult years of the war and occupation and was now becoming militant; it was demanding radical changes in the leadership, just as the second phase of the Communist uprising was about to begin.[4,5,6]

ΩΩΩ

---

4. Ibid.

5. Panotis, p. 44.

6. J. Theodorakopoulos, "Ho Oikoumenikos Patriarches Athenagoras ho A', Paneuropi-Hellenismos 15 (Sept. 1973), 13.

CHAPTER 1

ORIGINS, SOCIAL BACKGROUND, AND EDUCATION

1. Early Years

Patriarch Athenagoras was born in the village of Vassilikon in Epiros. His lay name was Aristokles and he was the son of Doctor Matthew Spyrou and his wife Helen, nee Mokoros.[1]

Patriarch Athenagoras never disclosed the date of his birth. He used to say, "I am an old man." To people of his own age or older than himself he always said, "You know, I could be your grandfather." He really kept his birthday a secret because it coincided with the day of the Greek revolution against the Ottoman Empire, the twenty-fifth of March.

He was very considerate towards the Turks. Although Greek by birth, he recognized certain qualities in the Turks, and he believed that

---

1. I. Panagopoulos, "Ho Patriarches Athenagoras Ho Megalos tes Orthodoxias," Christianos 131-37 (1972), 66.

the two countries should supplement each other and hand-in-hand walk
the path of peace and civilization. For this reason, he avoided cele-
brating his birthday in order not to be identified with Greek nationalist
parades. The Patriarch would say:

We used to live like Easterners. Our home was lit with oil lamps.
There were no chairs or beds, but large cushions and mattresses, which
during the day were rolled into bundles. When it got dark, we all sat
round the fireside sitting crosslegged in the Turkish fashion.

ΩΩΩ

The Patriarch's family, [writes Olivier Clement] belonged to the
powerful middle classes of those days, which were the flesh and blood
of Hellenism. The Patriarch's grandfather on the paternal side was
a shepherd. When Athens became the capital of the new kingdom
of Greece his grandfather went to Athens and became a butcher. He
prospered, and as a result, his son was able to study medicine. In the
Ottoman Empire, most of the doctors were Greeks and the Turks had
great respect for them. Later, Matthew returned to Epiros and so the
village of Vassilikon acquired its first doctor.[2]

The Patriarch had this to say about his birthplace:

Our village with about five hundred families was built on a wind-
swept plateau, which in winter was always snow-covered. My father was
a good doctor because he was well thought of by the villagers. In fact,
he seemed to be almost always on horseback as he had constant calls
from neighboring villages. My mother came from Konitsa, a larger village than Vassilikon, with almost fifteen hundred families. It was famous
for its shepherd's shoes, which I also wore.

During the Turkish occupation, the Church was, so to speak, the
Noah's Ark which saved our Greek language and culture. The Church

2. Olivier Clement, "Ho Athenagoras aphegeitai," To Vema (Feb. 9,
1972).

was liberal, unafraid of science, and believed that education would make religious faith more personal.

The Church appealed to the feeling of solidarity of the Christian people. The rich were expected to take under their protection all the intelligent children of the poor, and the teachers taught their pupils free of charge. In my youth, every parish had its own school and every town its high school. The high school of Yannina, where I was educated before going on to the Theological School of Halki in Istanbul, was famous. Yannina was in those days a great Hellenic center. It was a large, beautiful city with its cultural and musical organizations—a city uniquely Greek, where the Turkish judges and civil servants had to speak the Greek language in order to hold their positions. Behind the village of Vassilikon, on the top of a hill, was the traditional chapel of the prophet Elias. These chapels were always on the summit of a hill because the prophet Elias lived and prayed in the mountains, which themselves resemble the prayer of nature. Each morning, as you came out of your home, the first thing you saw was this lovely white chapel, and you got the wonderful feeling that you were protected by the prophet.

ΩΩΩ

During Athenagoras' childhood, Greeks held high positions in the Ottoman Empire. According to Clement, first Saves and later Alexander Karatheodoris Pasha were the foreign ministers of the Ottoman Empire. Some twelve ambassadors and representatives of the Sublime Porte were Greeks and among them was the famous Moussouris Bey. The personal physician of Sultan Abdul Hamid was also a Greek and so was the professor of medicine, who had been sent to Paris by the Sultan himself to study under Louis Pasteur. Some two million Greeks lived in the independent Kingdom of Greece, but more than eight million were within the frontiers of the Ottoman Empire. These Ottoman Greeks were not nationalists in the modern

sense of the word. They were more like the Byzantines. They had
kept alive the teachings of the Greek Orthodox Church because of
their religion rather than their Greek ancestry.

A whole, varied culture was seeking to express itself in modern
terms, [continues the Patriarch.] The Turks had literally fallen on the
Greeks like a thick layer of snow. Underneath that cold layer of snow,
however, there was warmth and vitality.

The area where I was born had been occupied by the Turks a
century before the fall of Constantinople. In my village, there were both
Turks and Christians, but we lived peacefully together; the Moslems were
invited to christenings and in their turn, the Christians were the guests at
circumcision feasts.

It was a sort of biblical co-existence and we all felt that we were
children of Abraham. The Moslems ate mutton and lamb during the
festival of Baihram and we Christians ate the Easter lamb. St. George's
Day was a great feast day. Quite near our home, there was a church of
St George which contained a very old icon of the saint. We used to climb
the hills to see the sunrise, and then after the church service, we used to
dance. On the same day, the Moslems celebrated the feast of Kidirle, the
feast of Al Kidr, while the Jews celebrated it as the feast of Elijah. So, at
least, said the dervishes.

The dervishes were very good to me, [continues Patriarch Athenagoras.] They were very tolerant toward the Christians and some of them
were well-known for their intelligence. We had one dervish in my village
by the name of Jamil. He often came to visit us at home and dine with
us. My mother and sister, in particular, were very fond of him and kept
no secrets from him. Jamil knew their innermost thoughts better than our
village priest.

His father, Doctor Matthew Spyrou, was a dignified man. For
this reason, he was a strict man. The Patriarch was physically unlike

his father, but in character, he was very much like him, especially in his self-criticism and his lack of vanity. Patriarch Athenagoras says of him:

My father was a pious man but in a discreet, introverted way. He never spoke about these things, but he always crossed himself before starting his meal, and he always went to church every Sunday. He was stern with us three children, but never hard. I was the eldest, then came my brother who was two years younger—he died in 1948—and then came my sister who was three years my junior. My father had a great weakness for my sister.

I have a photograph of my father which I always carry with me when I travel, but unfortunately none of my mother because in those days there were no photographers in the villages.

In Konitsa lived my maternal grandmother Efrosyne, one uncle whom we all adored, and an aunt, who sang beautifully the heroic ballads of the fearless Klephts—the bands of irregulars who fought the Turks—who still lived free in the mountains. During the vacations, we used to go to Konitsa where we always had an enjoyable time.

The person who taught us the meaning of religion and worship was, in fact, my mother. Every night when we went to bed she used to sing to us ecclesiastical chants and tell us about Saint Kosmas of Aitolia, who a century earlier had come to live at Vassilikon.

Saint Kosmas had founded ten high schools and over two hundred parish schools, among which was that of Vassilikon. Athenagoras admired Kosmas because of his principles—love for one another, a social consciousness, respect for women, a great desire for learning, and the conviction that the development of the individual inevitably leads to the strengthening of his faith.

ΩΩΩ

The Patriarch recalls:

At the Kosmas school I had a very attractive woman teacher. I saw her again in 1963 when I paid a visit to my village. She was then almost a hundred years old, skinny, almost blind, but still retaining her intelligent mind. I told her then that when I was her pupil, I thought she was very beautiful. She smiled, and, seemed a little disturbed by my confession. Then I told her she ought to be proud that she had educated a man of my position. Often you can judge the caliber of the teacher by the quality of his pupils. But, unfortunately, the old lady who lived in the house of my mother until her death, understood very little.

ΩΩΩ

After two years at the Vassilikon school, Aristokles Spyrou went to the school at Konitsa from 1895 to 1899. Suddenly in 1899, his studies were interrupted by a serious illness which almost cost him his life:

I was thirteen years old, [continues the Patriarch] when my mother and I fell ill simultaneously. I was so ill that I became unconscious and remained so for many weeks. When I got better I asked for my mother. My father explained that my mother was not at home, because he could not look after two seriously ill patients, and so he had sent her to her family in Konitsa. Impatiently I waited for the return of my mother. I was all skin and bone and my convalescence was extremely slow. But my mother did not return!

One winter's day I was sitting in the warm sun in our courtyard, when someone came up to me and asked "Does Matthew Spyrou, who lost his wife some time ago, live here?" The shock nearly killed me, but that is how I learned about the death of my mother. She had died three months earlier at the age of thirty-seven. I have never forgotten her. I will always miss her.[3]

ΩΩΩ

_____

3. Ibid.

Whenever the Patriarch spoke about his mother Helen, his eyes always filled with tears, and he seemed to gaze far into the distance. The very thought of his mother always tortured him. His sister explained it to me one day. "Mother died because of him, but he does not know it. I beseech you, don't ever tell him, because it will kill him." I kept my promise and never uttered a word, but I do confess that whenever I saw the Patriarch's eyes filled with tears, I became desperately unhappy. But, for men like him, who are perpetually prisoners of their position, tears are just part of their everyday suffering. That is why, even if you tried to exclude him from the house of a dead man, he would still go back in order to share the sorrow of the bereaved which he felt also belonged to him. The black robes he wore symbolized the bereavement of his people and also his own bereavement of his mother:

When my mother died, my sister was ten years old. Thanks to her courage and her good health—despite the hard life she led—and thanks to her faith in God, she took on the entire household and became a little mother to us all. I always remember that for three months after the death of my mother, my sister would climb up a hill and gaze at Konitsa, very much like the Moslems do when they say their prayers, facing Mecca. Only my sister was praying while gazing at Konitsa—the birthplace of our mother.[4]

ΩΩΩ

When he finished school in 1903 with the help of Chancellor Athenagoras, he entered the famous Theological School of Halki, in Istanbul. Several years later, aged twenty-three, he graduated with a degree in theology and was ordained deacon by Metropolitan Polykarpos of Elasson. Soon afterward he was appointed Archdeacon at the Metropolis of Pelagonia at Monastir. There he served with distinction until 1919 when the Metropolis was absorbed into the Serbian Church.

4. Ibid.

In an interview, the Patriarch said:

At Monastir, apart from one or two dreadful incidents, I had some wonderful experiences of the love of which simple people are capable, of dialogue, and of my first contact with Christians of the Western Church. I developed a strong personal contact with the local villagers, and each day, about a dozen of them would pay me a visit. When I asked them why they came to see me, they replied in their simple language, "So that we can look at each other." From this looking at each other I developed a practical philosophy: to love communication with men as I love men, as individuals, because in man I see God, and behind the miracle of human existence is God Himself.

In order to manage to communicate with the Catholics, I became a pupil at the school of the Marian Brothers, using as an excuse that I wanted to perfect my French. I sat at my desk and became very friendly with a gentle and very humble man, Brother Fideli, who was also my teacher.

I would like to emphasize once again that there is nothing more fulfilling than to be able to communicate with another human being. Conversely, the inability to communicate is one of the greatest human tragedies. If the world is divided today, this is largely due to the fact that people are unable to communicate and exchange views.[5]

In 1919 I left Monastir to go to the monastery of Mylopotamos on Mount Athos. Here I lived in the cell of Patriarch Joachim III together with Metropolitan Chrysostomos Kavouridis of Pelagonia, who at his death was known as the Archbishop of the so-called Palaiomerologites [or Old Calendarists][6] I lived at the monastery in complete isolation and in fantastic self-concentration, perhaps as a sort of penance

5. Panagopoulos, p. 66.

6. An ecclesiastical group that refused to accept the Gregorian Calendar and continued to follow the Julian Calendar, which is thirteen days behind the Gregorian Calendar.

for the atmosphere of hate in which I had lived. On Mount Athos, I felt
that a new world was being born and that God meant us to serve this
new world, and when I received two invitations, one from Metropolitan
Meletios [of Athens] and the other from the Metropolitan Gennadios
of Thessalonike, I decided to abandon the sacred silence of Athos and
to go to Athens as secretary of that great man Metropolitan Meletios.
I served him faithfully and wholeheartedly because I found Meletios a
true ecclesiastical leader. Unfortunately, this great man fell foul of the
political passions of his time. Meletios was indeed one of the first men
to see clearly the new realities facing the Church, which neither a new
mental attitude nor tradition could order or alter.

ΩΩΩ

So, in 1929 Athenagoras became Archdeacon of the Metropolis
of Athens under Metropolitan Meletios, who subsequently became
Ecumenical Patriarch and later Patriarch of Alexandria. Archbishop
Meletios (Metaxakis) of Athens—who is said to have influenced Athenagoras' attitude regarding administration and subsequently his very
personality—liked and respected the new clergyman so much that
he expressed the desire to take him with him to the United States.[7]
But Athenagoras refused because he disapproved of the incursion
of politics in church matters. He preferred to stay behind to serve
equally faithfully Theoklitos, who succeeded Meletios as Archbishop
of Athens.

Some months later, Athenagoras became the first secretary of the
Holy Synod of the Church of Greece and at the same time was pro-
moted to Archimandrite. He stayed in this position until 1922 when the
church hierarchy unanimously appointed him Metropolitan of Corfu
and Paxi, a position he filled with distinction.

7. V. Stavrides, "Ho Oikoumenikos Patriarches Athenagoras ho A',"
Stachys (1972), 308.

2. METROPOLITAN OF CORFU AND PAXI

With Meletios and his successor, Metropolitan Theoklitos of
Athens, we had few contacts with the other Churches—because of the internal problems at the time—except with the Anglican Church. When in
1922 I went to Corfu as Metropolitan, I was on very friendly terms with
the Catholics of Corfu and especially with their Archbishop Leonardo
Printezi, which in a sense was quite revolutionary in view of the then pre-
vailing attitude and psychology of the Greek clergy. Printezi and I used
to go out for walks together and we freely exchanged ideas and views. At
the time there were two rich goldsmiths in Corfu who were good friends
of the Archbishop. One of them was married to the aunt of an Orthodox priest and he used to come with me whenever I went on a visit to
the villages; many people began to think that I had converted him to the
Orthodox Church. I denied this, adding that I preferred him to remain a
Catholic so as to show that I was neither a fanatic nor a proselytizer.

But as I have already said, I had a lot of good friends among the
Catholics, the Protestants, and also among the Jews of Corfu:

The Jews once gave a reception in my honor. In the course of my
speech, I mentioned certain events that had caused their persecution and
I caustically condemned these anti-Jewish measures. As a result, the Jews
took a great liking to me, and on occasions when they had no rabbi they
used to ask me to handle their own administrative problems. They used to
pay me regular visits and every Saturday they came and had a talk with me.
Then we had a rather unfortunate incident. A young Orthodox boy was
lost, and it was rumored that he had been taken captive by the Jews. Fearful
of reprisals, Jewish businessmen shut up their shops and they and their
families remained indoors. I immediately called the chief of police and told
him that the child must be found as soon as possible, adding that I would
hold him personally responsible if any anti-Jewish incident occurred. I took

my stick and one of my priests and we went around to the Jewish quarter. The Jews indeed were in a panic, so I told them not to be afraid and that I would stand by them come what may. Well, the child was finally found, and believe it or not, he had gone to stay with some relatives in a small village outside of Corfu, and so that put an end to the panic. Yes, quite truthfully, the Jews were just as sad as the rest when I finally left Corfu.[8]

ΩΩΩ

One ought to mention Athenagoras' amazing action on 31 August 1923, when a unit of the Italian fleet shelled Corfu and killed dozens of people. Athenagoras, to the amazement of everyone, suddenly commandeered a rowboat and rowed himself out to the Italian flagship. He then went on board and confronted the flabbergasted Italian admiral with these words:

"I am obliged to congratulate you for your magnificent achievement. You, a civilized man, have killed with your indiscriminate shelling quite a few of my people, among them some refugees from the Asia Minor disaster. You know, Admiral, these poor people had taken refuge in Corfu after losing their homes and suffering untold miseries, only to be killed or maimed by your own shells. If you think this is bravery, do carry on with your shelling, Admiral."

ΩΩΩ

The Italian admiral was speechless. The courage and tirade of Athenagoras had an immediate effect. He ordered all ships to cease fire. Athenagoras possessed the personality and strength of character which had an immediate effect on people whether they were his friends or enemies, and the Italian Admiral was no exception.

Typical of the spirit he introduced into the Orthodox Church was the maiden address he gave as Metropolitan of Corfu on 2 March 1923. Among other things, he said:

---

8. Panotis, p. 46.

"Then, unfortunately, came the division of the Churches. Christ wanted one indivisible Church; instead, the Church became divided into factions. One must not hide the truth. The Church, which should have been the House of God, the Mother of all Christians, the Great Messenger of Peace, often forsook these principles and embarked on petty struggles, on missions of hate and persecution, and abandoned the people to their own fate without lifting a finger to help those in need, to help those who were sick or those who had been thrown into prison."[9]

ΩΩΩ

For these reasons, Athenagoras never denied his love and help to those who were outside the Orthodox flock. For example in 1923, following the Asia Minor disaster, a number of Armenians had also taken refuge in Corfu. They were a sad, unfortunate people—frightened, impoverished, leaderless—who had sought refuge in any part of the world. One day, a group of them came to him and begged him to give them access to a church and a priest to conduct Holy Communion. Athenagoras knew that there were certain differences between the Greek and Armenian Orthodox Churches, but in moments of crisis, he thought, one does not indulge in theological discussions. So, not only did he fulfill their request, but he himself officiated at the Holy Communion. In this way, the great believer in the unity of the Church carried out his first ecumenical action by allowing the blood of Christ to bridge the gap of the centuries. After that, he gave the Armenians a church and a priest, so that they could worship God in their own fashion and language.[10]

Equally typical was his attitude toward the Catholics. In Corfu, there was the Marolla family who had taken a great liking to the Met-

9. Ibid.

10. I. D. Skiadopoulos,"Apo ta pepragmena mias oktaetias," Apolytrosis 72-76 (1973), 18.

ropolitan. Athenagoras used to say that the Marollas were Orthodox in spirit, but Catholic in fact At any rate, this difference in dogma did not prevent the development of a warm friendship between the Marollas and the Metropolitan. In fact, the family expressed the desire to be converted to the Orthodox religion, but Athenagoras refused. He did not want people to say that he had used his personal friendship in order to obtain converts for his Church.

One of the saints especially honored by the Marolla family was a saint called Onoufrios. It seems that this long-bearded ascetic of Egypt had at some time or other performed a miracle for the Marolla family and as they were a very rich family, they expressed their admiration for the saint in various ways. The prime example of their generosity was the rebuilding of the Church of the Three Martyrs in Anemomylos— which was especially connected with St. Onoufrios and its subsequent financial maintenance by the Marolla family. On June 12 each year, the Marolla family celebrated the saint's feast day in great style. Several priests took part in the service, which was always conducted by the Metropolitan himself. Those, of course, who benefited from the feast day were the poor because on that day the Merolla family donated large sums of money to the Metropolitan for the sole use of all those in need.

Athenagoras himself was a great philanthropist. Philanthropy was a passion with him, giving his everything to the poor. To do this, he himself led a frugal life, and when his slender means were exhausted he would go and borrow money from the merchants and the bankers. Athenagoras was indeed proud to be poor, and his thoughts were always for those who were poorer than himself. To Athenagoras, the most humble beggar was a personality, but when he gave alms, even to such a humble beggar, he was always careful not to offend his feelings. He put in an envelope whatever was left of his salary and gave it to his faithful messenger Andreas Grammenos to distribute to the poor at their homes. Athenagoras' list for alms included even prostitutes. Instead of disowning them, Athenagoras gave them money and, what was even more important, tried to have them integrated into society. He did this by arranging marriages between the prostitutes and the men with whom they had had long associations. It is interesting to note that many of these married prostitutes subsequently became good mothers and created happy families.

His capacity for helping and doing good was endless. Sometimes he would meet a priest in the street wearing a worn-out robe or shoes that were in tatters. He would invite the priest to the Metropolis and there and then give him his own robes or his own shoes, or even his own umbrella.[11] This was the great joy of Athenagoras—to give, to do good. According to him, the greatness of man was not measured in terms of his possessions or his success, but simply by his good deeds. Real wealth was to have a loving heart and a constant desire to do good. Athenagoras was a true interpreter of the commandment of God: "Provide no gold, silver, or copper to fill your purse, no pack for the road, no second coat, no shoes, no stick; the worker earns his keep."

One day, children's voices were raised in the streets of Corfu, saying: "Refugees, refugees have come to the monastery of Saint Theodore." We all ran towards the monastery, and there in the square, we came upon a most moving sight. The entire square was filled with refugees from Cappadocia in Asia Minor and they were in a ghastly state. Their few possessions were piled on horse-drawn carts. While the refugees talked with the abbess of the possibility of being given asylum in the monastery, the cart drivers were making a fuss because they wanted to return to the port in order to bring back another group of refugees. The situation was definitely getting out of hand. Fortunately, at that moment, Athenagoras arrived with a priest They all fell to their

11. Ibid., pp. 25-26.

knees, crossed themselves, and looked up at the great-robed figure in awe. He spoke to them with great gentleness and asked them to remain quiet and at peace. All talking and noise ceased. Quietly he told them that he had already made arrangements for a number of homes to receive them and to look after them. And so in a matter of minutes, Athenagoras successfully solved the problem for the monastery, which could not have accommodated such a vast crowd of refugees.

I also remember that later on, he transferred the Corfu orphanage to the monastery. There was a great number of orphans in Corfu in those days, and Athenagoras himself looked after them with such paternal and Christian interest that he soon became their hero.

Athenagoras, however, was not always a heroic figure, because reality forced him to mix freely with the people. But even then, he was titanic in his modesty. He wanted to find "the beautiful moment" and to say to it, "Stop, don't go away!" so that he could enjoy that moment; but alas, that beautiful moment always eluded him. He could never be an ordinary individual, but always a leader who with humility had to lead his people along the right path so that they could fulfill themselves. When he woke up each morning, he prayed that on that particular day he would at least be able to offer some hope to those in need.

He was a man so full of love that he wanted to embrace everyone, the whole of humanity, despite the fact that his inner thoughts were disturbed by the tragic cry of the Bible, "My God, my God, why hast thou forsaken me?"

For this reason, you often saw the enactment of biblical-style scenes in the streets of Corfu. Just as the mothers of Galilee took their infants to Christ to bless them, so did the women of Corfu go out into the streets and wait for Athenagoras to pass by. Then the women would gather around him, asking him to bless them and their children. Forgetful of time and often of an important appointment back at his office, he

would take the children into his arms and kiss them and bless them and
talk to the mothers about their daily problems and give them advice
and encouragement. Nor was it unusual for the Metropolitan to open
up his wallet and gently and without fuss press a note into the hand of
some needy woman.[12]

3. HIS OTHER WORK

In 1923, he succeeded in reopening the Ecclesiastical School of
Corfu, and towards the end of the year, he participated for the first time
in the Athens Conference of the Hierarchy of the Greek Church.

In 1924 he founded the Corfu school as a state orphanage, and
he started publishing the journal Saint Spyridon—the patron saint of
Corfu. This incidentally was the first journal of the Orthodox Church
in Greece and its main aim was to show that the Greek Church was a
living and active institution. The profits from the journal were given
each year as a dowry to a young bride without means.

One of his greater achievements was the successful organization of
the beautiful Cathedral of St Spyridon where the remains of the saint are
kept. These remains, strangely enough, were bequeathed to the old Voulgaris family, but Athenagoras managed to persuade the family to cede
their rights to a church committee especially created for this purpose.
From that day onward the Cathedral of St Spyridon became completely
self-governing. At the same time, he made several improvements and
alterations to the Cathedral. For example, he installed pews and carpeted
the floor of the church, which consisted of large stone slabs that during
the winter months made even the most devout Christians shiver with
cold. For this action and for installing an organ in the Cathedral, Athenagoras was, unfortunately, criticized as being too much of an innovator.

---

12. Ibid.

Athenagoras was also very active in the creation of communal cemeteries. He disapproved of graves being placed in the center of villages or in churchyards because he thought their custom was unhygienic, and therefore he transferred all cemeteries to the open country. So it is thanks to Athenagoras that today all cemeteries in Corfu are situated outside all villages and towns.[13]

On 27 July 1923, a general assembly of the clergy of Corfu and Paxi was called under the presidency of Athenagoras. One hundred and twenty-five priests attended. In the course of his address, the Metropolitan stressed that the success of the Church largely depended on a fuller understanding of the rights and responsibilities of the clergy both towards the Church and towards the people themselves. He laid down certain rules: that parish registers should be properly kept, that churches should be kept orderly and clean, that sacred icons should be thoroughly maintained, and that all priests should abide by the rules and regulations of the Church, but in the spirit of modern times.[14]

Athenagoras remained as Metropolitan in Corfu for eight years. During this period he took part in two Christian Youth Assemblies, one held in 1926 in Helsinki, and the other in 1932 in Cleveland, Ohio. In 1930 he took part in the preliminary committee of the Orthodox Church at Mount Athos and he represented the Church of Greece at the Sixth Assembly of the Church of England which was held at Lambeth Palace, London.

Then in 1930 came a new challenge for Athenagoras. On August twelfth of that year, the Ecumenical Patriarch appointed him Archbishop of North and South America—an area where the Greek Church was plagued by inter-communal disputes generated by bitter conflicts

13. Ibid., pp. 11, 17.
14. K. Bones, "Athenagoras ho A' ho Oikoumenikos Patriarches," Ekklesia 49 (1972), 397.

over Greek politics. The people of Corfu were dumbfounded when they
heard the news of his appointment No one really wanted to believe this
report, and various contradictory reports and rumors started to circu-
late among the villages and towns of Corfu. Finally, to put a stop to any
further misunderstandings and disappointments, Athenagoras officially
announced the decision of the Patriarch and at the same time fixed the
date of his farewell service.

On that Sunday the Cathedral of St. Spyridon was filled to
capacity. But the strange thing was that the congregation consisted
of every religious denomination under the sun—Orthodox, Catholics, Protestants, Jews, Armenians, and even Moslems, who had come
across from Epiros to hear the farewell address of Athenagoras. The
occasion resembled the threnos and lamentations of a Good Friday
service. When Athenagoras started his farewell address, people fell to
their knees and tears began to fill their eyes as they listened to the last
moving words of their beloved Metropolitan. When the service ended
and the last kiss of peace was exchanged, men and women mobbed the
Metropolitan. They kissed his hand and received from him the blessed
bread (antidoron) which they were to keep as a last momento of their
departing Church leader.

Athenagoras left Corfu on 17 September 1930 on a ship named
Poligos. Two hours before the ship was due to leave harbor, people
began to flood the quayside. Meantime Athenagoras was preparing to
leave the Metropolis. In attendance were all his clergy, representatives
of the armed forces and police, and high-ranking officials. As he descended the marble steps of the majestic building, Athenagoras suddenly stopped, knelt down on the last step, and with great emotion kissed
the marble stone. He then rose and began to walk towards the harbor.
As he walked, men, women, and children rushed up to him to say goodbye and to kiss his hands or his robes. Athenagoras, deeply moved and

full of dignity and love touched their heads and blessed them. A little while later, he stood. on the bridge of the ship, a silent giant of a man who could not hold back his tears. As the ship's siren gave three blasts, thousands of white handkerchiefs began to flutter and wave frantically and people began to shout: "Please come back, please don't forget us." The grey-bearded giant stood erect and silent on the bridge of the ship, watching, staring, taking everything in, trying to imprint forever on his inner mind that last unforgettable sight of Corfu and of his beloved people—Christians, Jews, Moslems—because for Athenagoras all of them were the people of God.

ΩΩΩ

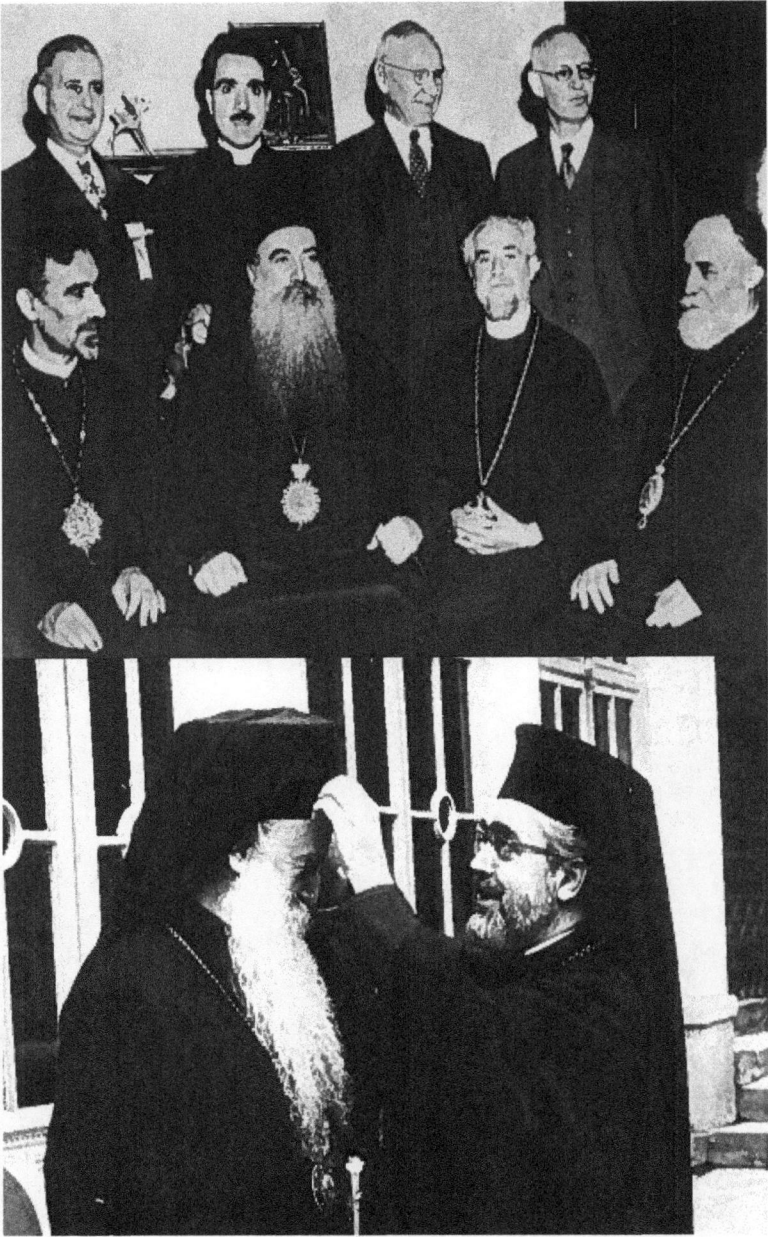

CHAPTER 2

ARCHBISHOP OF NORTH AND SOUTH AMERICA

1. THE BEGINNING OF HIS MINISTRY AS ARCHBISHOP

Athenagoras was the ideal man to send to the faction-split Greek community of America. During his eighteen years of office in America, he succeeded not only in bringing unity to the Greek community but also in giving it status and renown. When he arrived in the United States on 24 February 1931, he immediately declared that the Church was neither pro nor anti-Venizelist. The Church wished to see the Greeks of America living in peace and unity and not divided by political hatred. "I have come," he said, "to serve the community as a whole, and not to ally myself with groups or organizations. The Church's mission is to become the mother of everyone and to love and understand people irrespective of their political affiliations."[15]

---

15. Panotis, p. 39Z.

His regular visits to all the Greek churches in America gave him the opportunity to get to know the United States and to bring a closer and better understanding between the Royalist and Venizelist groups. He used to say, "Leave your political discussions and differences outside the church. When you go out of the church, you can always pick them up again."

The former Archbishop of Athens, Hieronymos—who incidentally was never an admirer of Athenagoras—made the following comment:

In America, Athenagoras found thousands of Greek immigrants who were deeply divided over their political loyalties, which, unfortunately, they had brought over with them from the mother country. He inherited Greek communities which because of these hatreds lacked the incentive and will to cooperate and were incapable of implementing any policy directive. Eighteen years later, when he left America, he handed over to his successor a highly organized Archdiocese, consisting of hundreds of disciplined parishes, efficient lay committees, an ecclesiastical school for its priests, a school for Greek teachers, and above all, with all Greeks of America united and pulling together for a common cause and the good name of Greece.[16]

ΩΩΩ

There is no doubt that with the departure of Athenagoras from Greece, the mother country suffered a great loss, but the Greeks of America gained a great man. Typical of his activities, energy, and enthusiasm was the building of hundreds of Greek churches in the United States and the creation of three hundred schools, cultural and social clubs, and community centers. But perhaps his most important achievement was the meeting of the Fourth Clergy-Laity Congress of

16. Archbishop Hieronymos, "Athenagoras ho A,"Ekklesia 49 (1972), 394.

the Archdiocese of North and South America in 1931, which voted a new constitution. Among other things, the new constitution laid down that all resolutions should first receive the approval of the Ecumenical Patriarch. It initiated the principle of auxiliary bishops and created regional administrative councils, each of them working under the chairmanship of the bishops, ultimately responsible to the Archbishop. At the same time the Assembly—which included representatives of the three hundred Greek communities—unanimously declared its belief in the welfare and future of the Greek Orthodox community of America. It is interesting to note that this administrative system, which was conceived by Athenagoras, continues to be in effect today.

In addition, Athenagoras organized every type of communal activity from matrimonial and divorce tribunals to church schools, from educational centers to communal newspapers. In 1931 he created the Greek Women's Philanthropic Society with branches throughout the United States. In 1937 he founded the Theological School of the Holy Cross, first at Pomfret, Connecticut, and later in Brookline, Massachusetts. Finally, in 1944 he established in Garrison, New York the St Basil's Academy for the education of teachers and choir directors.

Perhaps one should again emphasize that when Athenagoras assumed his position as Archbishop there were one hundred nineteen communities in America; when he left in 1948, their numbers had increased to three hundred fifty.

Athenagoras untiringly traveled throughout the United States, going from town to town, from city to city, trying to imbue the Greeks of America with the love and spirit of the Greek Orthodox tradition and to revitalize their pride in their Hellenic ancestry. His presence and his words always had a tremendous effect. Soon the Greek communities began to work together in harmony and to discard the political differences which for years had divided them and weakened them.

In this way, Athenagoras carried out the mission entrusted to him by the Ecumenical Patriarch, Photios II, that the Greeks of America should once and for all resolve their political differences and put an end to their long-standing quarrels. But to achieve this, Athenagoras often had to use harsh tactics such as recommending to the Patriarch the removal or dismissal of certain priests from their parishes:

But the harshness of Athenagoras was always tempered with patience, understanding, and love. Many clergymen, like the writer himself, were often determined to oppose the Archbishop; but when they came face to face with him, they found themselves completely disarmed because his reasoning was always just, and his attitude always reflected the great Christian values. The love in his eyes, the beauty of his language, the tenderness in his deep voice, and all the other natural gifts which enriched his superb personality were always at the disposal of the Church and of its people.[17]

ΩΩΩ

Finally, it is fitting to recall the words of Eleanor Roosevelt, the wife of President Roosevelt, when she laid the foundation stone for the new Greek cathedral in New York. "The Greeks," she said, "who immortalized their ancient glory with so many magnificent temples, now express their love for their adopted country by building and consecrating this great Greek cathedral in New York."

2. PAN-ORTHODOX, PAN-CHRISTIAN ORIENTATIONS

After achieving the unity of the Greeks of America, Archbishop Athenagoras began to look further afield toward the unity of all Christians. He worked extremely hard to achieve a rapprochement with other Orthodox Churches in America. In March 1935 a service was

---

17. Panotis, p. 39Z.

held in the magnificent church of the University of Chicago. While the seventy-two church bells peeled their joyful notes, three thousand Greeks, Russians, Serbs, and Romanians filled the church, and their choirs chanted in turn in their own language. Athenagoras himself adds this comment:

Denominational differences must be finally resolved because these differences belong to the past. This was my message; then it was heard and understood by our Orthodox brothers of other nations; and later, Catholics and Protestants began to understand it also. Such is the strength of the love of God.

I shall always remember a spontaneous event which took place in Boston in the summer of 1947. We gave a dinner in honor of Greece. Among the guests was the Catholic Archbishop of Boston, Richard Jacob Cushing, who in 1958 became Cardinal. When we met we embraced each other in front of everyone, and photographers took several pictures. The next day, some three thousand American newspapers carried this photograph on their front pages under the title "The first embrace between the East and the West."[18]

ΩΩΩ

3. NEO-BYZANTINE CULTURE

As a preacher, Athenagoras was not great. He looked upon preaching as a sort of complement to the service. On one hand, he wanted his sermons to have a touch of the heavenly, but on the other, he thought it was essential for a sermon to deal with the vital problems of the day and to offer some sort of solution to them. He wanted the Church to be the armor and the shield of contemporary Christianity. Love means sacrifice. That is what Christ demanded from the rich

---

18. Bones, p. 402.

young man, who although a law-abiding citizen, was nevertheless not
sure that he would enter the Kingdom of Heaven. So he asked Christ
how he could fulfill his wish, and Jesus said to him: "If you wish to go
the whole way, go, sell your possessions, and give to the poor, and then
you will have riches in heaven, and come and follow me."[19] But the
young man did not do this, because he loved his wealth and was a slave
to material things, although he was a law-abiding citizen.

This was also the reason why Athenagoras loved Paul, who in his
first letter to the Corinthians said:

I may speak in tongues of men or of angels, but if I am without
love, I am a sounding gong or a clanging cymbal. I may have the gift of
prophecy, and know every hidden truth; I may have faith strong enough
to move a mountain; but if I have no love, I am nothing. I may dole out
all I possess or even give my body to be burnt, but if I have no love, I
am none the better.[20]

ΩΩΩ

Finally, Athenagoras achieved a great deal thanks to his personality and to his superb qualities of leadership; he came to be
esteemed and respected not only by all Orthodox and other Christian
denominations but also by the American government itself. All great
political, ecclesiastical, and cultural personalities of the world came
to visit him and often sought his advice. This enhanced the reputa-
tion and prestige of the Greeks of America. I myself saw a saintly
Russian bishop, who was considered to be one of the great figures
of the Orthodox world, stand in front of Athenagoras and behave
as a pupil does to his teacher. I have seen foreign politicians respect-
fully bend to kiss his hand, Athenagoras gently withdrawing it and
embracing them instead. The giant of the Greek Orthodox Church

19. Matthew 19:20
20. 1 Corinthians 13:1-3

was like a real grandfather, embracing and kissing his beloved grandchildren. Archbishop Athenagoras II of Thyateira and Great Britain writes:

> When he left the United States, he had an overdraft at the bank of one hundred dollars. He literally left America with one robe and one pair of shoes and a broken umbrella. He had given all his belongings away. I know this for certain because I personally put his affairs in order.[21]

ΩΩΩ

---

21. Archbishop Athenagoras of Thyateira, p. 436.

CHAPTER 3

ECUMENICAL PATRIARCH

1. THE BEGINNING OF HIS MINISTRY AS ECUMENICAL PATRIARCH

On 1 November 1948, following the resignation for reasons of ill-health of Patriarch Maximos V, Athenagoras was elected Patriarch by the Holy Synod. He became the 268th Ecumenical Patriarch of Constantinople and New Rome, and a leader of the entire Orthodox Church under the name of Athenagoras I.

It has been said that his election was influenced by American, Greek, and Turkish policies. This is not true. The Greek government was against the appointment of Athenagoras, as I was told by the then Under-Secretary of State Panayiotis Pipinelis. Athenagoras, wishing to emphasize his independence from political pressures, told me: "All officials who from time to time appeared to support me, became my enemies when they suddenly realized that I was not willing to play their game."

In this way, one can also explain why the accusation that he was pro-American was completely shattered after the first Pan-Orthodox Assembly of Rhodes. After this Assembly, the Russian Orthodox Church not only ceased her attacks against the Ecumenical Patriarch but recognized the Patriarch as leader of all Orthodox Christians. This, of course, gave rise to a new rumor that Athenagoras was pro-Russian. In actual fact, the Patriarch had neither favorites nor secret allies. It is true that he had a great liking for the Russian Church and that he was very fond of the Orthodox Slavs, but it is equally true to say that he accepted Turkish citizenship which was forced upon him by his position, and at the same time continued to express his admiration for the American way of life. Therefore Athenagoras was equally friendly with all nations concerned.

2. EXPECTATIONS-CONTRADICTIONS OF BYZANTINISM AND COSMOPOLITANISM

Athenagoras flew from New York to Istanbul on 26 January 1949. He arrived on the personal aircraft of the President of the United States, which President Truman had put at his disposal to honor him. Some one hundred fifty thousand Greeks went to the airport and gave him a tumultuous reception. They saw in him a man who had the full support of the United States, a man who was strong and a well-known fighter, but also a man who was ready to avenge all the wrongs committed by the Ottoman Empire against the Greeks. They even expected him to convert almost overnight Haghia Sophia into a Christian cathedral again!

Naturally, they were soon to be disappointed, because instead of preaching a policy of hatred, vengeance, and discrimination, Athenagoras sent forth a message of friendship and unity, not only to the other Christian Churches but also to the Turks themselves. Soon most of those who had gone to the airport to cheer him and greet him with olive branches started to change their tune. They began to talk against him, and some of them even referred to him as 'the nylon Patriarch'; they laughed at him when he put pews in the churches and were deeply shocked and offended when they heard that he had gone to pray in a Moslem mosque. Athenagoras, however, was unshaken in his determination to see that the Greek Orthodox Church was brought into line with contemporary Western thought and attitudes. He could not see how the pseudo-romantic ideas of Byzantium could fit into the modern Western world. He was aware that philhellenism—a product of the nineteenth century—stemmed from a sort of abstract love and admiration for ancient Greece; for that reason, he often said: "The focus of this feeling was always the Parthenon, but never Haghia Sophia." Byzantium and Haghia Sophia had been enveloped in the mists of history and destroyed by papal dogmatism.

Unfortunately, few people understood Athenagoras' thinking, because the insular and isolated community of a hundred and fifty thousand Greeks still lived in the past, in the political and ideological climate of the First World War. As V. Th. Stavridis, professor at the Theological School of Halki put it:

From the very first it became obvious that Athenagoras, with his wide and liberal background acquired in America, was not going to follow the narrow and prejudiced concepts of the ecclesiastical tradition of the Phanar. He brought with him to Constantinople the enlightened spirit of the Western world, and he was determined to implement his policies with all the energy and enthusiasm that characterized him, but he also expected all those who worked with him to adopt the same standards and to strive for the same objectives.[22]

ΩΩΩ

---

22. Stavrides, p.312.

His assistants at the Phanar, however, were not yet ready for such drastic changes. It was therefore no surprise that when he was enthroned as Ecumenical Patriarch, the ceremony was a strange mixture of Byzantine grandeur and American modernity. The presence of Greek-American advisers, not to mention President Truman's personal plane, gave the strong impression that Athenagoras had the backing of a great nation, which brought to mind a parallel event—the assumption of leadership by Prince Alexander Ypsiliantis of the 1820 revolution in Wallachia and Moldavia (present-day Romania). In his address from the throne, the Patriarch said:

I send forth from this Ecumenical Throne a message of hope, through faith in God for a better tomorrow… We believe that only through religion and faith in God will men live in peace with each other because religion is eternal beauty because religion is the majesty of peace. This in fact means that it is not enough to be an idealist; man needs an iron Christian will to achieve these ideals. In order to enjoy the full beauty of Christian life one needs to believe and practice the spiritual and moral values of the Church.

ΩΩΩ

3. THE NEW TRADITION OF THE PHANAR

The Patriarch's address became the new message to the Orthodox world. It proved once again the power of the Patriarchate when in the hands of a capable and inspired leader.

At this point, one should pause to say a few words about the Patriarchate at the Phanar and its tradition. Metropolitan Meliton of Chalkidon put it this way:

The Patriarchate at the Phanar is the very nerve center of the entire Orthodox world. It symbolizes the ability of man to overcome catastrophe, to extract some good from the worst. It is the champion of high principles and moral values, it is the emblem of patience, silence, and nobility. It is the guardian of our faith and of our sacred tradition of the East, always vigilant, always dynamic. It is the gateway from the West to the East and the sensitive receiver of communications from the West. The Patriarchate is a great institution and the Phanariot clergy are the custodians of a great heritage preserved for the advancement of the Orthodox peoples. But while maintaining tradition, they are also sensitive to progress, in order to be able to adjust to the realities of a given situation.[23]

ΩΩΩ

4. HOMOS POLITICS?

That was the tradition that Athepagoras wished to revive in modern terms. He sincerely believed in Graeco-Turkish unity and friendship, not in order to protect American interests or those of any anti or pro-Soviet power, but simply because he wanted to see the Greek and Turkish people become masters of their own fate and not to continue to exist as the poor dependents, the lackeys, of the great powers. He thought that Professor K. Sfyris' theory—that Greece must never allow herself to pursue an anti-Turkish policy—was the correct one.

In the context of his past experience, he considered that the independence of Turkey was vital, and he was highly critical of any policies that would exploit the Greek population in Turkey for military purposes. He considered that such a policy would not only endanger the existence of the Greek community but would also affect the independence of Turkey itself. He believed that a Graeco-Turkish union might well lay the foundations. He thought that the area between the Russian steppes and the sea was controlled by Eastern Europe; Eastern Europe itself was controlled by the Balkans, and the Balkans, by the area between MoraviaAxios-Egnatia. Therefore, by virtue of their position,

23. In Panotis, p. 57.

the Balkans and Asia Minor were vital areas in the maintenance of the balance of power. For the sake of world peace, it was unthinkable to disturb the swing of the pendulum between the Middle East and the Balkans.[24] He even entertained a union of Greece and Turkey on the pattern of neutral Switzerland. He thought that such a union would benefit the interests of the superpowers much more than the constant confrontation of each other across the Dardanelles.

Within the new dual-nation, the Greeks, being a sea-faring nation, could have developed their activities in the European, Asiatic, and Atlantic areas. At the same time, the free movement of populations and the development of the economy within the Aegean area would have acted as a brake on any shallow, chauvinistic ideas. In his view, a real Graeco-Turkish union would have altered the whole future of the two nations and would have been the most significant political event since the fall of Constantinople in 1453.

But visionary though he was, he failed to appreciate two important factors: *(1)* that such a revolutionary idea would presuppose the backing of the West and *(2)* it would presuppose an enlightened leadership in both Greece and Turkey which would espouse the cause of internationalism as opposed to nationalism.

This in fact was our point of disagreement when I went to visit him at the Phanar in March 1950. He spoke, as usual, with great warmth about Graeco-Turkish friendship and outlined to me his hopes and expectations. My reply was:

You are quite right, Your Holiness; the Greek and Turkish people are united by a bond of friendship. But do please remember that the urban class of New Turkey, which came into power after the Kemal revolution, and took over the positions held by Greek merchants,

24. K. Sfyris, Hypo poles pro ypotheseis he Hellas einai yiosimos? (Athens, 1931), p.67.

industrialists, and civil servants during the Ottoman Empire, would be strongly opposed to a Graeco-Turkish union. I am afraid they would fight bitterly your idealistic concept of such a union.

ΩΩΩ

His eyes suddenly narrowed and I sensed an impatience and a cloud of anger creep over his face. He pressed the bell on his desk and his secretary came in. "Please be good enough to show our guest out," he said drily, "because he wants to leave."

Early next morning, I received a telephone call from his secretary, saying that His Holiness would be most happy if I could have breakfast with him. I took a taxi to the Patriarchate, and within a few minutes, we were sipping our morning coffee. After a few preliminary pleasantries, he said, "You know, you caused me to spend a sleepless night. In fact, I didn't sleep a wink. However, please be good enough to repeat your argument."

This time, with greater tact and politeness, I analyzed and went more deeply into my various arguments. The Patriarch listened with patience and he was visibly depressed by the indisputable logic of my theories, but he tried to hide his disappointment with these words. "Yes, I think I understand; but please promise me not to repeat these words to anyone else."

"Rest assured, Your Holiness," I replied, "what I said will remain within these four walls. It was meant for your ears only, my Ethnarch."

What really can be drawn from this account is the fact that the Patriarch was a wise and most knowledgeable man. But cold logic by itself had no great attraction for Athenagoras; only great ideals like peace and Christian brotherhood filled him with enthusiasm. He always wanted to elevate the more mundane events of history to the lofty heights attained by the spirit of freedom. As Andreas Kalvos said in one of his poems: "Death is far sweeter if one falls from a great height."

5. BASIC OBJECTIVES

On becoming Ecumenical Patriarch, Athenagoras set himself four objectives.

One: the reorganization of the Archdiocese of Constantinople and of all the dioceses outside Greece.

Two: the preservation of complete pan-Orthodox unity and real cooperation.

Three: cooperation with all Western and Eastern Christian Churches. This would eventually lead to the unification of all Christian Churches, once certain practical considerations were satisfactorily worked out.

Four: the peaceful and harmonious existence of the people of the eastern Mediterranean through the creation of dual and multi-national federations, in order to combat racial discrimination and social injustice.

We must remember that Athenagoras was the first Patriarch who did not believe in nationalism of any kind. He maintained that the primary psychological result of the Asia Minor disaster of 1922 was that the Great Idea had been completely shattered, and a void had taken its place. The pan-Hellenic ideal of the Great Idea,[25] which was shared by all Greeks, irrespective of culture, social status, and political beliefs, had ceased to exist. The Greek people no longer believed in Greece, which was without a leader, but they continued to believe in Hellenism. The highest ideal of the Greek people and the justification for their existence was from then on based on Greek culture and civilization. The new Great Idea had to be something different: the creation of a dynamic neo-Hellenic spirit which would continue the great traditions

---

25. That is, the re-establishment of the Byzantine Empire with Constantinople as its capital.

of Greece, but would at the same time adapt itself to modern conditions, be receptive to Western and Eastern thought, and finally with positive work and creative ideas project that neo-Hellenic spirit beyond its national frontiers.

If it were possible for me to summarize the real objectives of Athenagoras, I would put them in these words: from the moment that Hellenism ceased to be on the defensive with the motto "Every non-Greek is a barbarian," it passed into its aggressive/creative phase. (Aggressive policy was also the policy of Isocrates, who said, "We consider all those who participate in Hellenic culture as Hellenes.")

Such, in brief, was, I think, the policy of the inspired leader of the Greek Orthodox Church, which incorporated the ideals of the brotherhood of man, freedom of thought, and solidarity between the nations of the world.

6. POLITICAL DIFFERENCES BETWEEN ATHENS-ANKARA

This policy of Athenagoras was violently criticized by conservative political elements in Greece after the Turkish riots in Istanbul on the nights of 6 and 7 September 1955, when Greek property was burned and looted by Turkish extremists. Unfortunately, these dramatic and historical events and the worsening relations between Greece and Turkey caused by the grave Cyprus crisis made the work of the Patriarch extremely difficult. But the worst of all was that the conservative Greek establishment, influenced by pseudo-romantic and escapist ideas, was unable to learn any lesson or face the realities of the disastrous campaigns of 1897 and 1922. The Greek establishment not only rejected the Patriarch's policy for a confederation with Turkey but refused to follow the elementary policy of Graeco-Turkish friendship, which after all was the policy laid down by the great liberal leader of Greece, Eleftherios Venizelos.

I do not wish to deal with the relative responsibility of the Turkish leaders of the time, because this is their own affair. I am only concerned with the responsibilities of the Greek leaders. But it must be remembered that Athenagoras never accepted the official Greek policy. He was the first Greek Patriarch to visit the Turkish President and other political leaders in Ankara in 1949 and again in 1952, and during the same year, he received the Turkish Prime Minister Adnan Menderes at the Phanar. But stupidities on both the Greek and Turkish sides were responsible for the tremendous suffering of the Christian population of Istanbul.

The cause of it all was, of course, the Cyprus issue. Often, when Athenagoras was asked what he thought of Archbishop Makarios, he used to reply:

Quite frankly, I can't understand how an Archbishop can become responsible for the death of men. Nor do I believe that Greece can ever defeat Turkey, Britain, and America. And you know how much I love my country, but one must be a realist These are facts, and we have to face them.

ΩΩΩ

When I visited Archbishop Makarios in 1961 I asked him what he thought of Turkey? He replied: "I do not know of such a country." I think that similar witticisms, lacking in what one might call European consciousness, encouraged Turkish fanatics six years earlier to burn down one hundred churches belonging to the Ecumenical Patriarchate.

Incidentally, when Athenagoras saw some of these churches burning, he told me that at that moment he felt deeply ashamed of the civilized world. He stayed indoors, feeling not anger, but just sorrow, but he avoided making any rash decisions which might have undermined the historical position of the Patriarchate. This prompted irresponsible people to say that the Patriarch should have rushed out into the streets

and 'hit a few Turks on the head.' One day when we were alone, I
referred to this criticism. He replied with great simplicity:

I am an old man, and therefore it would be easy for me to become
a martyr. All those who seek posthumous glory somehow always want to
become martyrs, but my office and my responsibilities forbid martyrdom. At any rate, I think that those who wanted me to become a martyr—meaning the then Greek government—wished to see me sacrificed
in order to redress their own wrongs and conceal their own weaknesses.

ΩΩΩ

For Athenagoras, however, a theatrical death—which he would
certainly have met had he gone among the frenzied rioters—would not
have been martyrdom. For him torture was to remain alive and to see
the desecration of his churches; torture was to witness the incredible
policies of self-deception of the Greek and Turkish governments and
to read about the so-called 'attitude of realism' adopted by the other
Christian Churches. Torture for him was also the recollection that for
years he had proclaimed to his followers: "Do not be afraid, because we
are law-abiding, disciplined, and united under God. We are not alone
because by our side stand millions of our other Christian brothers."

It is also interesting to note that several Greek governments—especially those after Alexander Papagos—tried to throw responsibility
for the tragedy of the Greek community in Istanbul upon the Patriarch.
Athenagoras, on the other hand, maintained that only states are responsible for breaches of international law when these breaches are the
direct result of their external and internal policies. It is a little early to
judge whether this clash of views was based on ideological grounds or
simply resulted from a personal bias against Patriarch Athenagoras.

At any rate, the clash of Greece and Turkey over Cyprus had a
catastrophic effect on the Patriarch's pan-Christian policy. The breakdown of his policy of Graeco-Turkish cooperation also affected the

future friendly relations he wished to develop with other Christian Churches. Meanwhile, the petty opposition displayed by other Balkan countries was greeted ironically by all the great international organizations of the world.

7. THE TRIAL OF ADNAN MENDERES

There is no doubt at all that Athenagoras' breadth of mind was far removed from the pettiness and cruelty of our times. This was once again demonstrated by his behavior when he was summoned to be a witness at the trial of Adnan Menderes, the Turkish Prime Minister who was responsible for the anti-Christian campaign in Turkey. The President of the Military Court—which had the audacity to call him as a witness—had in his possession an important letter which the Patriarch had sent to Menderes, containing these words: "If you, Mr. Prime Minister, do not offer indemnity for the damage caused by the riots to Greek property, I shall come to the conclusion that you personally are responsible for the persecution of the Orthodox Church."

This vital document was found in Menderes' briefcase when he was arrested by the Turkish revolutionary officers. The President of the Military Court, after informing the Patriarch that the document in question was in his hands, ordered the Patriarch to be sworn in. Pale but dignified, Athenagoras rose to his full height and took the oath. Then the President asked him, "Do you know the accused?"

The Patriarch cast a benevolent, almost paternal look at Menderes, and gently replied, "Of course I do."

The President then asked, "Can you tell the Court who was responsible for the events of 6 September 1955?"

The Patriarch replied politely, "It is you, Mr. President, who must answer that question. I endured the riots; I did not organize them."

The Military Court was placed in an awkward position. If the Patriarch had disclosed the role that the Menderes government had played in the riots, he would have certainly incurred the hate of the majority of the Turkish people, who had always faithfully supported Menderes. If, on the other hand, he had spoken against Menderes himself, he would have antagonized the susceptibilities of the Moslems. Athenagoras, however, as a true Christian did not wish to harm anyone, he preferred to remain a witness without blood on his hands.

Athenagoras gazed for the last time at the condemned Menderes with gentleness and concern. For a moment Menderes looked back at the Patriarch with respect, then he lowered his eyes, as if out of shame. I am certain that Athenagoras at that instant would gladly have given Menderes the Kiss of Resurrection. Such was his greatness and strength that even at the most stormy and trying moments of his life, he always managed to remain calm and composed and pursued his Christian principles without ever wavering or giving in to weakness, ill-feeling, or temptation.

8. PAN-ORTHODOX UNITY

At the end of World War II, the Patriarchate of Moscow was obliged to toe the line of Soviet policy in return for a quasi-independence granted to it by the government. The Soviet government placed at the disposal of Patriarch Alexisan airliner, and he and his retinue made several trips to the Middle East with the excuse of visiting the various Patriarchates. These frequent visits to the leaders of the other Orthodox Churches—to whom generous gifts were always made—had three objectives in view: to give the impression to the people of the Mediterranean basin that within the Stalinist regime a great and holy Russia continued to exist; that the New Russia was willing to support and protect the Orthodox Churches of the Middle East; and lastly, that the Moscow Patriarch, as the de facto successor of Byzantium, was the alternative Ecumenical Patriarch.

We must remember that the vision of a free and worldwide theocracy, which would protect all the oppressed peoples of the world and unite all Christians under the protection of Moscow, was a Slav ideal that had first germinated in Russia in 1473. Dostoevsky himself had declared in 1880, that "Every Russian is a brother soul and that the mission of the Russian brother soul is to work peacefully towards the spiritual union of mankind."

Professor Ugo Rahner, speaking in Austria in 1949, drew attention to the fact that the spirit of Caesar had magically hovered over the Kremlin after Patriarch Alexis had declared in 1947: "Today Moscow is the hope and protection for all nations that love and cherish peace."

On the other hand, the meeting of Russian bishops in Paris on 29 September 1945 pointed out: "The time has now come when the Ecumenical Throne in Constantinople should no longer be filled by a Turkish subject." This in fact meant that Stalin's Russia was not only trying to create a Third Rome but was seeking to capture the Second Rome (Byzantium) which ought not to be governed by a 'Turkish subject," but by a Slav.

It is also interesting to note that the official journal of the Russian Patriarchate carried the following comment: "Moscow is the Third Rome, and our fathers have taught us since the time of Ivan III that there was no Fourth Rome." This, of course, I repeat, meant that by the creation of the so-called Third Rome, the Second Rome (Constantinople) was entirely superseded. Two different tactics served the same strategy for the new triumph of the Russian Orthodox Church now that Moscow had become the co-capital of the world and one of the nerve centers of world power.

For precisely that reason the renowned Byzantine scholar of Munich, Franz Dolger, noted the following:

If we observe that the Moscow Patriarch is trying to impose himself as the leader of all Orthodox Churches of the world, this is simply a revival of the policy enforced during the Middle Ages, and whose objective was the supremacy of the Russian Church with the object of establishing an entirely new society.[26]

ΩΩΩ

That this policy is pursued today is shown by the fact that the post-war textbooks in Russian high schools contain no important ecclesiastical historical dates, yet they quote the important phrase of monk Philotheos of Pskov: "Moscow is the Third Rome and a Fourth does not exist"

If we add to all this the polemical articles written by Professor Trotsky which denied the predominance of the Ecumenical Patriarchate, it becomes obvious that Athenagoras ascended his throne under the very opposition of the Church of Moscow. In 1948, Professor Trotsky had accused Athenagoras that his objective was to subjugate and Hellenize all the non-Greek Christians who lived outside the jurisdiction of the autocephalous churches. In other words, he accused Constantinople of imposing a dictatorship. In fact, the Moscow Patriarchate, thanks to the opposition of Athenagoras, had failed on the occasion of its five-hundredth anniversary to convene a meeting of the pan-Orthodox pro-Synod with the view to taking over the leadership of Orthodoxy. The scheme of Moscow was to enforce a voting procedure by which the representatives of the autocephalous churches would have no votes, and in this way, the ultimate decision would be made only by the bishops forming the pro-Synod.

26. See U. Rahner, Vom Ersten bis zum Outten Rom (Innsbruck, 1949), p. 18.

Meantime, Metropolitan Germanos of the Ecumenical Patriarchate had during the first years of Athenagora's leadership published
several articles attacking the Russian Professor Trotsky. Athenagoras,
of course, true to his character, regretted that such an attack had been
made because deep down the Patriarch had a genuine admiration for
the Russian Church—during the Russian Revolution it had gone into
hiding and had emerged strengthened at the end of the World War II.
So he was happy, though somewhat hesitant to publish a study of mine
on the Russian Patriarch Alexis and his Church.

Athenagoras was of the opinion that in a gigantic country like
Russia, religion was the only language through which people could
communicate with each other and with the outside world. Religion
was also the only means of keeping together the Russian Orthodox
Church, the other sister Orthodox Churches, and the mother Church at
Constantinople. He believed that Russian Orthodoxy could not be suf-
focated by a political dictatorship and by the same token, the Orthodox
Church in general would never cease to carry out its duty in helping
and guiding people toward a better Christian future.

Finally, he believed that Orthodoxy would never benefit from internal clashes. He intensely disliked all political speeches which caused
disunity in the Churches. He considered that in comparison with
pan-Orthodox unity, capitalism and Communism were second-class
institutions. Nevertheless, for the sake of ecclesiastical convention, he
was willing to accept the post-war policy of co-existence. He himself
called several pan-Orthodox meetings in which he gave a place of hon-
or to the Patriarch of Moscow without, however, being able to alter his
rank—he was fifth in seniority—in the Church hierarchy. The ecclesiastical axis Constantinople-Moscow did not reflect so much the policy
of detente between Washington and Moscow but demonstrated the fact
that Orthodoxy could place itself above national-racial differences and

produce ecclesiastical unity under clashing socio-political regimes. In addition, the pan-Orthodox front strengthened and facilitated the Eastern Church to become a sort of bridge between the Catholic and Protestant Churches. In this way, the Church in its role as a spiritual power could limit the influence of each country by assuming the leadership of the peoples of the world in the pursuit of peace and concord.

Whereas in earlier years Moscow had questioned the right of Constantinople to convene pan-Orthodox Assemblies, Moscow now formally acknowledged and welcomed it. One of the reasons for Moscow's change of mind was the visit of Patriarch Alexis and all the other Patriarchs and Archbishops of the Eastern Church to Constantinople. In addition, the Ecumenical Patriarch's triumphant visit to the Holy Land and the enthusiastic reception accorded to him by the other branches of the Eastern Church and their followers confirmed that the head of the Eastern Church was definitely the Greek Ecumenical Patriarch of Constantinople. Incidentally, Athenagoras was deeply concerned that he was unable to pay a return visit to Alexis, the Russian Patriarch in Moscow, although this was due entirely to circumstances beyond his control.

At any rate, the international press considered that the greatest achievement of Patriarch Athenagoras was the re-establishment of unity between the Orthodox Churches. Before he became Ecumenical Patriarch, the other Orthodox Patriarchates and heads of the autocephalous Churches had little or no contact with each other, except at Christmas and Easter when they exchanged greetings. These tenuous and causal relations between the Eastern Churches began to have dangerous repercussions after World War II when the Soviet Union for obvious political reasons tried to impose the Russian Church as the leader of Orthodoxy in the Eastern World. Patriarch Athenagoras counteracted these Machiavellian tactics by organizing a series of

pan-Orthodox assemblies. It was indeed a great historical event when
in September 1961 he succeeded in convening a meeting in Rhodes of
the representatives of all the Orthodox Churches and of all the Eastern
Churches as far as India at which a declaration of unity and common
purpose was made. The representatives of these Churches had not met
since the years A.D. 879. Only a man of the caliber and personality of
Patriarch Athenagoras could have achieved the task of bridging the gap
of eleven centuries!

9. DISRUPTION OF THE PAN-ORTHODOX FRONT BY THE CHURCH OF GREECE

Strangely enough, the Church that put up the greatest opposition
to Athenagoras' policy was the Church of Greece itself. All of its Archbishops except one challenged his policy of pan-Orthodox friendship
and cooperation and made vicious personal attacks against him: that
he was pro-Protestant, pro-Catholic, pro-Turkish, a Freemason, and a
dozen other groundless accusations calculated to discredit and deni-
grate the Patriarch. The Archbishops of the Church of Greece became
almost hysterical in their efforts to emaciate the Patriarchate of Constantinople and to transfer its power to Athens. Needless to say, such dis-
sensions were of great benefit to the Soviet policy because conflicts and
divisions within the Eastern Church would only result in making the
Church in Russia stronger than the Church in Greece. But even more
serious was the fact that the opposition of the Church of Greece to
Constantin9ple created difficulties for the Western World. Is it possible
to visualize a conservative institution like the Church of Greece going
counter to Western policy and thus supporting the interests of Moscow?
And yet, this is exactly what happened, consciously or unconsciously,
during the twenty-two years of Athenagoras' rule.

Even this openly hostile and disruptive action of the Church of Athens did not affect the calm and magnanimous nature of Athenagoras; he just smiled and said: "I feel very sorry at the foolishness of the Archbishops of the Church of Greece." He could, of course, have retaliated by immediately bringing the churches of central and northern Greece under his direct jurisdiction, as he was perfectly entitled to do because the administrative power of Athens extended from the Peloponnese up to the area of Lamia only.

At this point one should explain that out of seventy-seven dioceses formally subject to the jurisdiction of the Patriarch of Constantinople, forty-two are placed under that of the Holy Synod of bishops, which is presided over by the Archbishop of Athens and of all Greece. But Athenagoras, lacking the dictatorial touch, did not wish to take such action, and as a result the militant bishops and archbishops, undisturbed, continued their campaign of vituperation and defamation. Athenagoras, however, was gratified when he saw that the Slav and Arab (Antioch) Patriarchs expressed their solidarity with him during a period when successive Greek governments, prompted by their archbishops, accused him of being a revolutionary and on certain occasions even an enemy of Greece.

I remember the well-known journalist Mrs. V. Sgourdeos saying to me: "Your people in Athens conduct a persecution campaign against the Patriarch because they are petty and small-minded. They have much to gain by Athenagoras' policy, whereas he in turn derives no advantage. But they are so stupid that they can't see beyond their noses."[27]

The antagonism of the Church of Greece to the Church of Constantinople should also be seen in the following context.

One: the opposition of the Church of Greece was also opposition to the only remaining ecclesiastical expression of the Great Idea, which

27. G. Theotokas, Pneumatikeporeia (Athens, N.D.), p.48.

was politically impracticable but emotionally acceptable. Therefore the proclaimed nationalism of the Church of Greece was bogus.

Two: in the last analysis, it helped the promotion of a Third Rome, i.e. the institution of an Ecumenical Patriarchate in Moscow.

Three: the ecclesiastical nationalism of the Church of Greece was utopian because the Church of Greece came tenth in the hierarchy of the Orthodox Churches and therefore could never assume the first position. The argument that the followers of the Church of Greece were greater in number than those of the Church of Constantinople was not only false but again tended to support the Patriarchate of Moscow, which had a numerically larger flock, and to foster the ambition of the U.S.S.R. to transfer the Ecumenical Patriarchate to Moscow or, alternatively, to facilitate the occupation of the Patriarchate in Constantinople by the Russian Orthodox Church.

Professor Vezanis and Ambassador Triandafllidis, expressing the viewpoint of the Church of Greece, supported the old contention propounded in the 1830s by Theoklitos Pharmakides, the protagonist of the autocephalous Churches. According to Pharmakides, it was belittling for the bishops of the new Greek Kingdom to be subservient to an Ecumenical Patriarch to whom a Turkish Sultan dictated. On the other hand, Basil Laourdas and the author defended the Ecumenical Patriarch by emphasizing that the Church was not national, but ecumenical. They also pointed out that the Church of Athens was not founded by the Apostle Paul as a national Church, and that the history and tradition of almost two thousand years of Orthodoxy are in fact the history and tradition of the Ecumenical Patriarchate. But the naive, parochial, and fanatical nationalism of the Church of Greece resulted in the Church becoming autocephalous in 1850. Later the Churches of the Christian Arabs, the Serbs, the Romanians, the Bulgarians, and the Albanians followed suit and also became independent of Constantinople. In this way, the Ecumenical Patriarchate lost ground not only in the Middle East but also in the Balkans and in Eastern Europe, all of which was to the advantage of Moscow and to the disadvantage of the West.

I repeat, the accusation that the nationalism of the Church of Greece was petty and contemptuous was perfectly true, but this was perhaps to be expected because in its isolation and narrow-mindedness; the Church of Greece was obviously naive and unaware of the world-wide implications of its actions. But it is more difficult to understand and justify the sophisticated and certainly more mature Western powers, which at the time failed to give adequate support to the Orthodox people and to the Patriarchate of Constantinople.

Yet despite all these greatly disruptive influences and conflicting events, Patriarch Athenagoras was successful with his own policy and came out of the fray victorious. His first great triumph was the convening of numerous pan-Orthodox Assemblies in Rhodes. These conferences demonstrated beyond doubt that despite ideological and political differences, the pan-Orthodox Churches could meet and work harmoniously together. In this way, Athenagoras gave proof to the world that his Patriarchate was not only called ecumenical but was ecumenical in fact Perhaps the only ones who were unaware of these important implications were the Church of Greece and the Western powers!

10. RELATIONS WITH THE PROTESTANT CHURCH

One of Athenagoras' ambitions was to be able to work closely with the Protestant Churches. He looked upon the Council of Churches in Geneva as a sort of pan-Christian United Nations organization. He visualized it as a huge roundtable conference at which representatives of all the autocephalous Churches of the world would deliberate and exchange views. He thought that Bishop Iakovos of Malta, later Archbishop of North and South America, was the ideal representative

of the Ecumenical Patriarchate at the Council of Churches. Just as he
wanted the creation of a radio station on Mount Athos to broadcast
the message of Christ to the whole world, he also desired to see an
international church pulpit in Geneva from which the sermon of true
Christian solidarity and love could be preached. He believed that the
Protestants would be able to give a new impetus and direction to this
Christian solidarity, and unity. Moreover, he believed that together the
Protestants, Catholics, Orthodox, and those of other denominations, by
drawing courage and inspiration from Christian ideals, would fashion
a new world in which love, friendship, and cooperation would triumph
over hate, prejudice, and discord. Athenagoras looked especially to the
Protestants for help, as he considered them to be less fettered by dogma
and because he admired their sincerity and their down-to-earth ap-
proach. For this reason, he had great hopes for the Council of Churches
at a time when his own position was being threatened by the breakdown
in Graeco-Turkish relations. It was only natural that after the Turkish
riots of the 6th of September 1955 he could no longer rely on the support of the Greek government. In fact, he was completely disillusioned
with Athens. He himself told me that when the Greek-charged affairs
in Ankara handed over the Greek demarche to the Turkish Foreign
Ministry, he had a broad smile on his face.

The Council of Churches, however, gave him considerable support during those tragic and very difficult days when law and order
had broken down in Istanbul. The German Protestants also came to
his aid; with a deep sense of Christian responsibility and European
solidarity, the Germans made a strong protest to the Turkish government, and to this was added the equally strong protest of the Anglican
Church. So the 'Protestant' Athenagoras, forsaken and abandoned
by the Orthodox Greeks, accepted the helping hand of the Protestant
Christian world. Incidentally, the Russian Orthodox Church, fearing

the disapproval of the Soviet government, did not offer any support; likewise, for political reasons, the Church of Rome also remained impassive.

The only contribution of Moscow was in fact a broadcast which said: "The question of the transfer of the seat of the Ecumenical Patriarchate is not a simple matter that can be settled between Greece and Turkey."

On the other hand, what did Greece do? Despite the fact that there was an all-powerful Church of Greece and numerous active Christian organizations, not one complaint was made to the Turkish government about the destruction of the Greek churches and the desecration of the remains of the Greek Patriarchs, which were taken from their tombs by the rioting crowds and burnt in public places. Nor was there an all-night vigil at any of the churches of Athens—an event which strangely enough happened years later when Pope Paul and Patriarch Athenagoras met in Jerusalem. The Orthodox Greeks made no public protest against the Turkish sacrileges. "The Greeks," as the writer Alexander Papadiamandis said, "have ceased to be Byzantines." Could one say in this case that the Protestants had become the Byzantines?

11. RELATIONS WITH THE VATICAN

Athenagoras, as you may remember, had already established good relations with the Catholic Church when he was Metropolitan of Corfu. He improved these relations when he became Archbishop of North and South America.

There is an interesting story about this desire to establish a closer relationship with the Pope when he became Ecumenical Patriarch. On his first flight to Istanbul in 1944, while his airliner—President Tru-

man's private aircraft—was flying over Rome, he requested the pilot
to circle twice over the Vatican. He did this in order to be able to pray
over the area of the Holy See. Athenagoras did not feel, however, that
the time was yet ripe for having a personal meeting with the Pope; plans
to do this were put in motion later.

In 1952 the Patriarch sent Archimandrite Emilios Tsakopoulos,
the librarian of the Patriarchate, to study librarianship at the Vatican.
The Archimandrite, who was an Italian scholar, was very popular at
the Vatican and he remained there for about a year. In the meantime,
the Patriarch was using various other means to establish contact with
the Holy See. As go-betweens, he used the distinguished Romanian
theologian Archimandrite Skrima and several other personalities of the
Catholic world.

The first official contact with the Vatican took place on 17 March
1959. On that day Archbishop Iakovos of North and South America
arrived at the Vatican and was ceremoniously conducted to the private
office of the Holy Father. Pope John XXIII rose from his chair and
warmly embraced the Greek Archbishop. Here is a record of their
conversation:

Archbishop Iakovos: "Your Holiness, I am deeply honored to be able
to convey in person the message of His Holiness the Ecumenical Patriarch. The message is as follows"

"'There appeared a man named John, sent from God; he came as
a witness to testify to the light, that all might become believers through
Him.' He quotes from John the Apostle because he believes that Your
Holiness is the second Apostle John, entrusted by God to carry out His
wishes."

"Patriarch Athenagoras believes that the assembly of Bishops of
the Roman Catholic Church at the Second Vatican Council was called
by God through the lips of Your Holiness. The Patriarch believes that

through love, this powerful unifying force, Your Holiness will make all roads lead to Rome—Rome, where belief in God was first proclaimed, signed, and sealed with the blood of thousands of Christian martyrs."

"This is the message of the Patriarch, a message of renewed faith, hope, and love. I am entrusted to deliver this message to Your Holiness, together with the Patriarch's prayers that this message might become the substance of unity in the divided, but One, Holy, Catholic, and Apostolic Church."

"The Patriarch would be happy to be assured that Your Holiness is indeed a man of God."

Pope John: "Today salvation has descended upon this house. I have a feeling that God Himself has visited this house. And indeed He has. Tell His Holiness that I believe that we are all the envoys of God. He more than I. The New Rome has sent you to us, the Old Rome. The Patriarch has anticipated me. I had in mind to send a representative to His Holiness in order to explain to him the reason for convening the Second Vatican Council—not a formal letter, as happened in the case of the First Vatican Council. Formal communications unfortunately do not always divulge the good intentions. It is time that we adopted a more direct method of communication. The object of the new Council is the re-union of the Church."

Archbishop Iakovos: "With your permission, Your Holiness. We hope that the old concept of unity—return to the Catholic Mother Church to be united—which was put forth at the First Vatican Council in Florence will not be advanced again at the Second Vatican Council. It is time we said, 'We must unite, but we must unite in all humility and prayer, because those who drink from the cup of love of Christ, must also be the first to unite under Christ'"

Pope John: "The union will be the union of hearts and of prayer. Communication with each other is the seed of unity. The slogan of the

French Revolution—Liberty, Equality, Fraternity—must prevail, other-
wise, there will be neither peace between nations, nor unity between the
Churches. Please repeat these words to His Holiness and convey to him
my gratitude and my brotherly love. And finally, convey to His Holiness this message, 'We are all envoys of God. Our mission is to prepare
the people for a dialogue of love; we must work hard with this object
in view until this dialogue becomes a prayer, and this prayer finally
becomes the union of the Churches.'" [28]

ΩΩΩ

This meeting between Pope John and the Greek Archbishop
Iakovos was the first formal meeting between representatives of the two
Churches since May 1547, when Pope Paul III received the Exarch of
Patriarch Dionysios II, Metropolitan Mitrophanis of Caesarea, who
subsequently in 1565 became Ecumenical Patriarch under the name
Mitrophanis III.

Now let us turn the pages of history and deal with a more recent
event, which has been interpreted in various ways. The year is 1959.
On June 11 of that year the President of the Turkish Republic, Jelal
Bayiar, visited Pope John XXIII. The object of the Turkish President's
visit was not to disrupt the pan-Christian front, because on the one
hand Patriarch Athenagoras had declared himself in favor of Graeco-Turkish cooperation, and on the other, the Vatican had no intention
of converting the Turks to Christianity. No, the visit of the Turkish
President had other motives, namely, the pan-Christian movement
against international Communism, and possibly the start of a rapprochement between Turkey and the Vatican. At any rate, there was
no Turkish intention, as some reports suggested, to begin a campaign
against the Ecumenical Patriarchate because this again would have
meant a victory for Moscow. The diplomatic contact between the Holy

28. Panotis, pp. 41-42.

See and Turkey was simply to discuss the transference of the seat of the papal representative from Istanbul to Ankara—after ninety-two years. (1868-1960).

When the Vatican later announced that the Second Vatican Council was to meet in Rome in 1962, the distinguished Roman Catholic theologian, Jean Danielou, made the following comment:

The Latin and Byzantine worlds with their respective interests have long ceased to exist. The dogma is more or less a common one, their traditions are similar and today their opponents are mutual. The centuries that have passed have created various prejudices which must gradually disappear. The first step, I think, is psychological re-adjustment.[29]

ΩΩΩ

12. THE JERUSALEM MEETING

The meeting between Pope Paul VI and Patriarch Athenagoras in December 1964 in Jerusalem represents a landmark in the annals of ecclesiastical history. I was fortunate enough to be in Jerusalem during this great historic event because I was a member of the Patriarch's retinue. Some two thousand international press correspondents had descended upon Jerusalem, and their main objective was to cover the movements of the Pope in the Holy Land, rather than the meeting of the Pope with the Greek Patriarch. "The press had made a great mistake because they did not know the caliber of Athenagoras," wrote Spyros Alexiou. The journalists witnessed the Pope's arrival at the airport, and then most of them went off to cable and broadcast their reports. Only a few stayed behind to meet and welcome Patriarch Athenagoras. When he

---

29. Ibid., p.-92.

alighted from his aircraft, the journalists were immediately impressed
by the tall, imposing figure of the Patriarch, who with his long, white
beard resembled the statue of Moses by Michelangelo. Excitedly they
surrounded him and fired questions at him, which he answered with his
usual charm and simplicity.

Press: "Why have you come to Jerusalem, Your Holiness?"

Patriarch Athenagoras: "To say 'Good Morning' to my beloved brother, the Pope. You must remember that it is five hundred years since we
have spoken to each other!"

Press: "And what about the differences between your Churches?"

Patriarch Athenagoras: "Where there is love and understanding, there
are no differences of opinion."

Press: "Do theologians agree with this?"

Patriarch Athenagoras: "I do not know, because there are many theologians. All I know is what theology says, and there is but one theology."

ΩΩΩ

The journalists were delighted with the interview and rushed to
Jerusalem to cable their newspapers and journals. The rest of the press,
who had followed the Pope, found that His Holiness was somewhat
aloof and reticent. Realizing their mistake, they too went in search of
the Patriarch in the hope of getting an unusual and colorful interview.

I must recount an incident which remains very vivid in my memory. It concerns the Pope's return visit to Patriarch Athenagoras which
took place at the residence of the Patriarch of Jerusalem. The Pope
had arrived twenty minutes before his scheduled appointment, and the
Patriarch was still not fully robed. Nervously I knocked on the door of
his dressing room and informed the Patriarch that the Pope had arrived
ahead of schedule. For a man of his size and age, he moved remarkably
quickly, and in one minute flat, he was out of his room and rushing to
meet the Pope. They embraced each other and I suddenly realized how

slight in stature the Pope was. He was literally engulfed in the arms and
the robes of the giant Athenagoras. For a few minutes they exchanged
greetings, and then hand-in-hand they walked into the ceremonial
rooms to meet their retinues and members of the press who were
waiting for them. After various introductions and exchanges of civilities,
the two great leaders stood side by side, and read in turn the Sermon
on the Mount—first in Latin, then in Greek. Finally, they retired to a
private office, where they had a conversation which lasted about twenty
minutes. When the Pope eventually left and I was alone with Patriarch
Athenagoras, he turned to me and asked, "Well, what did you think of
it—was it a success?"

I replied: "Your Holiness, it was the most liberal meeting that
has ever taken place between the leaders of the Western and Eastern
Churches. Neither you nor the Pope counted the number of bishops
and professors in each other's retinue nor did the meeting have the cut
and thrust of the Council of Florence. The look on the faces of the
bishops of the two Churches had nothing of that vacant seriousness of
the past You were all so human, such simple Christians—although you
are bishops of the Church—so please allow me to say that your meeting
was the most frank and the most open-minded meeting ever held between the leaders of the two Churches"

The Patriarch laughed heartily at my terribly serious description
and then said, "Nevertheless, we did achieve something positive today,
didn't we?"

I thought that he was very reticent at the moment of his great triumph. While the international news agencies and the television services
had waxed lyrical over what they called, 'the most important meeting
of the century,' Athenagoras remained modest, reserved, and perhaps
cautious. He was conscious that in the course of history man undergoes
many changes of heart, and events are often misinterpreted and dis-

torted. He had simply succeeded in bringing together the two Churches
that had been divided by mistrust and hatred for each other ever since
the year A.D. 1054.

I believe that even when Athenagoras sat on one of the two
thrones in the Vatican—a second throne of equal dimensions to that of
the Pope's had been brought in, especially for the occasion—he must
have smiled as he thought about human vanity. Theologians had always
maintained that there was only one throne, that of the Pope. But Athenagoras attached no importance to the fact that he had sat on a second
identical throne. To him this was mere exhibitionism; such things were
important only to ambitious and vainglorious men, and to be a good
Christian, or for that matter a Pope or an Ecumenical Patriarch, you
had to have simplicity and the purity of mind of a child. To him, real
wealth was not to be found in a position of power or money, but in
humility, love, and the ability to render service to mankind. Let others
criticize him, abuse him, and even accuse him of being a traitor to the
Orthodox Church. He remained untouched by all this because he knew
that schisms were not created overnight by ecclesiastical resolutions,
nor was the unity of the Churches accomplished by mere words and
embraces. Athenagoras had a great duty to perform, and he would not
deviate from the difficult, uphill road leading to his own ideals of Christian love and solidarity.

The Second Vatican Council was due to begin its work. Cardinal
Bea, head of the Roman Catholic delegation, requested that observers
of the Orthodox Church attend the Council. The Ecumenical Patriarch
put this request to the leaders of the autocephalous Churches. They
were not very receptive because already at the Pan-Orthodox Assembly
of Rhodes some of the bishops had expressed their irritation that they
had not been consulted about the Athenagoras Pope Paul meeting. After lengthy deliberations and hostile church demonstrations in Athens, it

was decided not to send observers to the Council. At the same time the Patriarchate of Moscow, always conservative and always anti-unionist, also gave a negative reply to Cardinal Bea. To soften the blow, Patriarch Athenagoras sent Bishop Emilios to the Vatican to explain in person the refusal of the Orthodox Church to be represented at the Vatican Council. Cardinal Bea conveyed this negative reply to the Pope, who was deeply upset.

Then the Vatican, desperately wishing to give a more representative character to the Second Vatican Council, sent a special envoy to Moscow in an effort to get the participation of the Russian Orthodox Church. The Patriarch of Moscow wavered but finally decided to send observers to the Vatican Council.

It has been said that the Vatican succeeded in its efforts for two reasons: one, it put pressure on the Church of Moscow through the U.S.S.R. government, and two, the Council took place at a time when the Vatican had decided to put an end to the unrealistic and useless cold war against Communist Russia and accept some sort of co-existence with the U.S.S.R.

Nevertheless, the achievement of the Second Vatican Council was not the participation of the observers of the Russian Orthodox Church. The real success of the Vatican Council in Rome was the announcement that Patriarch Athenagoras and the Pope had decided to withdraw the ex-communications (anathemata) of 1054 which caused the schism between the Eastern and Western Churches. Therefore, as the result of this historic initiative—which was brilliantly handled on the Greek side by Metropolitan Meliton of Chalkidon—the Second Vatican Council concluded its work with a positive, if not sensational, event which justified its convocation.

13. REVOCATION OF THE EX-COMMUNICATIONS

"We condemn the offensive words, the groundless accusations, and the reprehensible behavior which characterized the tragic events on both sides in the year 1054. We equally condemn and we excise from memory and the annals of Church history the resulting anathemata, memories of which to this day have poisoned relations between our two Churches and have prevented a rapprochement. We surrender these to eternal oblivion.

Finally, we express our deepest regret at these and subsequent events which caused the complete division of the ecclesiastical community."

ΩΩΩ

With these words, the Ecumenical Patriarch Athenagoras and Pope Paul VI, on 7 December 1965, announced to the world simultaneously from the Phanar and the Vatican their solemn decision to rescind the ex-communications of 1054. Nine centuries and eleven years had elapsed. The whole Roman Catholic Church, its clergy, and its flock applauded the decision within and outside the walls of St. Peter's Basilica.[30]

At the same time at the Phanar in Istanbul scenes of tremendous enthusiasm greeted the announcement and Greeks pressed forward to kiss the hands of Cardinal Sheenan, the Papal envoy—a sight not seen since the schism of 1054. Then the Patriarch and Cardinal Sheenan, who was also Archbishop of Baltimore and senior bishop of the U.S.A., bestowed a joint benediction on the crowd. So indeed, the annulment of the ex-communications was a milestone on the road to Christian reunion.

---

30. Metropolitan Chrysostomos of Myra, "He arsis tou anathematos," Poimen (1973), 69.

Now, let us briefly look back at the events of A.D. 1054. On 16 July 1054, during a service in the Cathedral of Haghia Scphia in Constantinople, Cardinal Umberto, the special envoy of Pope Leo VIII, placed on the high altar the ex-communication of the then Ecumenical Patriarch Michael. This was the climax of a long, bitter struggle of the Greek Orthodox Church against the domination of the Roman Catholic Church, which had started in the second half of the first millennium A.D.

The Ecumenical Patriarch then set a time limit of four days in which he demanded the withdrawal of the ex-communication. There was no withdrawal. After that, the Patriarch called together a council of the autocephalous Orthodox churches, which included the Patriarch of Antioch and the Metropolitans of Bulgaria and Cyprus. The Council decided to ex-communicate Cardinal Umberto and all those who had drafted the papal ex-communication of Patriarch Michael. At the same time, the Council decided to exclude all Latins from receiving Holy Communion in Orthodox churches.

This briefly is what happened in the year 1054 and which in the Greek Church came to be known as the anathemata.

Now, the question is, what was the result of the annulment of the ex-communications in 1965? Was the schism healed and was unity achieved? The answer is well-phrased in the words of the announcement:

We remain as two Churches which have their differences—in dogma, liturgy, history, administration, and other matters—differences which were created during the centuries by well-known negative factors. We intend to deliver these differences to the fruitful dialogue which our two Churches will conduct from now on, on equal terms.

ΩΩΩ

The Greek Metropolitan Chrysostom of Myra adds a sort of foot-
note to the announcement by saying "the differences will be solved only
by the purification of the mind and the correction of past mistakes."

So, a new period began in which some of the more difficult practical differences and problems were discussed and solutions were sought.
It required great courage and intelligence to tackle certain subjects,
for example, the disputed doctrinal questions, religious propaganda,
conversion, and so on. Cooperation was achieved in certain areas of
international importance, such as world peace, education, hunger, social
welfare, and the care of the disabled and handicapped people. But
the main problem was the uprooting of hate and suspicion; this could
only be done by gradually bringing together the people of the two
Churches so that they could examine their differences objectively and
without prejudice. But the ideal of unity which eventually would have
led to the union of the two Churches was not achieved. One can well
imagine that if cooperation was difficult in the social sphere, how much
more difficult cooperation was on subjects such as the meaning of Holy
Communion? Although various sincere efforts were made to solve these
differences, the essential mutual trust was lacking. Correspondence
between the Vatican and the Ecumenical Patriarchate clearly shows
that despite well-intentioned if grandiloquent dissertations, the vital
differences created by centuries of mistrust and prejudice were either
completely ignored or subtly bypassed.

Athenagoras, however, was sincere. On 22 November 1963, he
wrote to the Pope: "We cannot offer anything more valuable to each
other than mutual love and understanding," and he added, "let us sacrifice our life, so that the Kingdom of God may come upon earth." He
was also honest. The Patriarch asked that "a dialogue on equal terms"
should begin with a first meeting of all leaders of the Christian Churches at the tomb of Christ in Jerusalem. The symbolism was obvious. The

Pope, however, rejected such a large meeting, but accepted, as we have already seen, the Jerusalem meeting of the Patriarch and himself.

But let us be objective. What actually was the positive result of the meeting of the two leaders in the Holy Land? It must be remembered that they exchanged views on two occasions only: once, for fifteen minutes at the home of the Papal Nuncio, and a second time for twenty minutes at the home of the Patriarch of Jerusalem. This alone proves that the darkness of the schism of the churches was not yet fully illuminated by the strong light of love because this love had not yet taken root. The only interesting thing that had happened was that the Pope put on the Orthodox robes offered to him by Athenagoras which were embroidered with a picture depicting Christ as a Teacher. The symbolism was "I consider you an Orthodox Archpriest, but do follow the teaching of Christ in practice." Pope Paul, on the other hand, who was more practical in his symbolism, offered the Patriarch the holy chalice; this meant that the Pope was asking for the doctrinal union of the two Churches.

Perhaps my analysis of the events in question is a little exaggerated, and perhaps the statement made by Metropolitan Meliton of Chalkidon to the Pope on 15 February 1965 in Rome is more to the point: "We must slowly rebuild with friendly contacts and frank exchange of points of view what was destroyed by centuries of isolation of our two Churches." But the Patriarchal Encyclical of Christmas 1968 came like a thunderbolt:

During our meeting in Jerusalem, His Holiness the Pope and I exchanged gifts—a cross and a chalice—and during our meetings, we expressed the hope alas, if the people ever arrived at union without the participation of the Churches themselves! [He continued,] We seem to discuss trivialities while the world is changed by momentous events. Science is experimenting with the prolongation of biological life; at the

same time, death unhindered is sweeping the continents of Asia and
Africa. Where is Christ our Savior? Divided, we have turned Christ
away from us.

ΩΩΩ

The theology of the heart cannot be one-sided. We either have a
socialist Christian society—in which the stronger man lends a helping hand to his weaker brother—or we surrender to a cruel, polemical exchange of words which is unaccepted to the Christian people.
The ex-communications of 1054 were condemned in the Cathedral
of Haghia Sophia; Pope Paul and Patriarch Athenagoras sat on two
identical thrones in the Vatican, and the Pope and the Patriarch sat
down together to a meal—according to protocol, the Pope eats alone.
Nevertheless, I am not sure whether the hundreds of photographs,
dispatches, and frequent television reports which immortalized those
historic moments convinced the greater public that "the leaders of
the two Churches descended from their thrones to inaugurate a new
epoch—an epoch of love, equality, and co-existence until such time as
they could meet in the chalice of Holy Communion."[31] This was an
ideal which was very dear to Athenagoras himself. But if there was failure, it certainly was not the failure of the Patriarch. The responsibility
rather lay on the shoulders of that tightly-knit community of Medie-
val-like prelates—on both sides—who frustrated a closer relationship
between men and nations. Patriarch Athenagoras looked upon Christ's
saying "Love your neighbor as yourself" as an expression of personal
freedom, an expression of a man who severs the bonds that bind him to
egotism, pettiness, and self-interest. But the ability to justify the actions
of our neighbors and the desire to sublimate our ego must exist within
ourselves. Unfortunately, it did not exist.

ΩΩΩ

----

31. Panotis, p. 183.

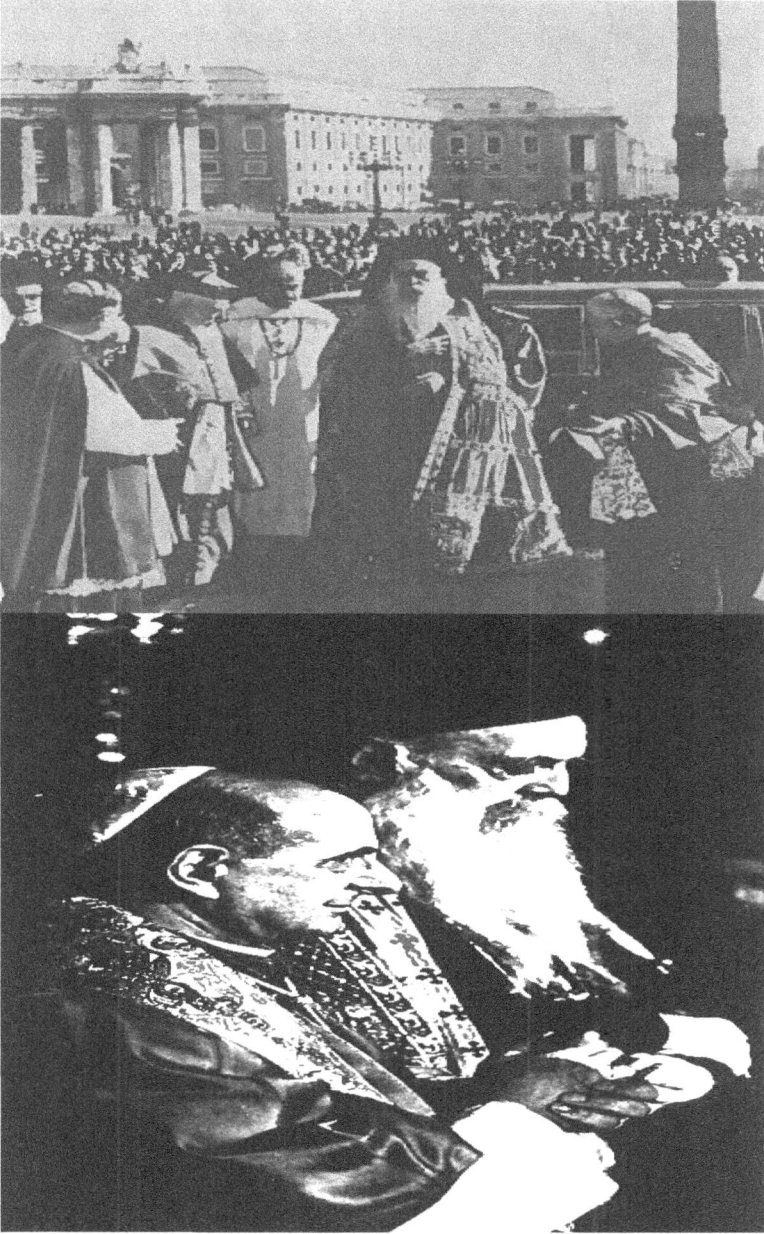

CHAPTER 4

THE PHILOSOPHY OF ATHENAGORAS

1.WAS HE A CHRISTIAN REVOLUTIONARY?

As a cleric, Athenagoras lived a life filled with one desire and one responsibility: to give real meaning to the Bible by interpreting Christianity not just as an esoteric philosophy, but as an actual modern way of life.[32] If he had not been a cleric, the Church with its medieval attitude would have excommunicated him a thousand times or more!

Athenagoras, like the heralds of the revolution of the peasant; like all those who wanted to bring the Church back to pure Christianity and the teachings of Christ, became a reformer of the Orthodox Church and the most sympathetic liberal of our times.[33]

The Church and the state realize that even the most genuine idealist gradually outgrows his theories as he begins to apply them and

32. Stefan Zweig, Ho kosmos tes Technes (Athens, N.D.), p.64.
33. Ibid., p.65.

that the most gifted and sincere reformers are usually those who cause
the greatest upheavals in society.

When Athenagoras started looking around him, he discovered
one of the most basic and obvious truths: that there is great inequality
in our society—tremendous contrast between the rich and the poor,
wealth and poverty.

In the course of his extensive travels, Athenagoras had already en-
countered poverty at close quarters, not only in the villages of his native
Greece but also in the industrialized, overpopulated cities of the United
States where poverty was the symptom of our times, the by-product of
our technological age. True to his biblical beliefs, Athenagoras at first
tried to help the needy with gifts and by organizing social welfare institutions; but he gradually realized that such personal efforts were useless
and that money alone could not change the tragic existence of these
unfortunate people.[34]

The Patriarch often reminded me of Leo Tolstoy. Tolstoy
wrote hundreds of pages in order to prove the contradictions of our
so-called civilized world: a world in which men carry out the orders
of the state to kill each other—contrary to the commandments of
God—and in this way place themselves, against their will, in situations
which their consciences disapprove of and condemn.[35] However, Athenagoras was a cleric, and he could not follow Tolstoy's concepts to
the ultimate end. He considered that each war—however short, with
all its bloodshed and its suffering, glorification of force and cruelty,
impressive parades and benediction of regimental flags, and all other
notable but hypocritical manifestations calculated to give a boost to
the morale of the warring nation—each war caused more amorality
in one year than the millions of murders and acts of arson and theft

34. Ibid., pp. 65-67.
35. Ibid., p.70.

perpetrated during the past centuries by individuals acting under the influence of passion.[36]

Athenagoras was once asked: "What has made you understand and love men so much?" He replied:

Hate! When in 1910 I went to Monastir—today it is called Vitoli in Serbia-I found myself in an atmosphere of hate. Greeks, Turks, Albanians, Bulgarians, Romanians, Jews, all of them were at loggerheads with each other. The only ones who had any measure of love were the Greeks and the Jews. I lived in this atmosphere of hate for eight long years. It is dreadful to hate and to want the destruction of another human being. It is abominable. This tragic experience became even more distressing during the 1914 war. In Macedonia, we had the armies of our friends and allies and of our enemies. Human life was worthless. Man was thrown into the cauldron of fire, not by his officers because his officers were good men. The murder was perpetrated by political expediency!

I saw men not only abandoned and scorned but treated like an animal. I saw the priests of the Orthodox Churches of the Balkans and the Churches of the West accompany the armies of their country; they marched with their soldiers, but they were incapable of standing amidst the fighting Christians and reducing, if not stopping, the violence, the bloodshed, the inhumanity that was going on around them because the priests themselves were living in an atmosphere of antagonism, schisms, and disunity. The hatred between men, the degradation of the great ethic, 'Love one another,' were responsible for making me the humble carrier of the love of God.[37]

ΩΩΩ

---

36. Ibid., p. 72.
37. Panotis, p. 45.

   And yet, Athenagoras was opposed to all the well-known revolutionary ideas of our time. According to him, the Christians believed
that all men are equal; the revolutionaries, on the other hand, wanted
to abolish inequality! The champions of class struggle, with whom he
often had lengthy discussions, always opposed the government in. power with help from outside. He also held the firm view that those wishing
to change the way of life of the world should first of all change themselves. For this reason, although he agreed with some of the aspirations
of the revolutionaries, at the same time he felt sorry to see them reaping
the advantages of an industrial society without distributing some of its
benefits to the poor. Athenagoras wanted a revolution of morals and
not a revolution of guns; he wanted a revolution of the conscience of
the soul and not a revolution of clenched fists.[38]

   Contrary to Tolstoy, Athenagoras considered that industry was in
the service of mankind. The great Russian intellectual did not travel by
train; Athenagoras did because he believed that technology brought about
various advantages, among them some personal freedom and leisure for
the individual. Finally, he did not find it necessary to wear the garments of
a peasant as Tolstoy did in order to prove his humility. He relied entirely
on his simple clerical robes, which after all were his only wealth. He had no
need to proclaim his humbleness because he was by nature an ascetic.

   His attitude towards the Catholic Church was completely objective
and without prejudice. This is well borne out by a conversation he had at
the Patriarchal Residence at the Phanar with the Dutch Cardinal Willbrans.

   "Your Holiness, what really caused the schism?" asked the Cardinal. The Cardinal was politely referring to the disputed doctrinal
differences between the two Churches. Athenagoras, without hesitation,
gave a very frank answer to the amazed Cardinal.

38. Zweig, p. 75.

"Saintly brother," he said equally politely, "the schism was not created by leavened or unleavened bread. The Holy Spirit exists in both of
these. The opposition was not theological, but entirely political. It was
the opposition of Rome to Constantinople. You represent Rome and we
represent Constantinople and Athens."

So we see that Athenagoras did not hesitate to put forward the
whole truth in contrast with the official communications and teachings
of the two Churches. He hated to mislead people with inaccurate facts
and historical falsehoods. On the other hand, he was always ready to
listen to representatives of Catholicism speaking their minds freely and
to discuss with them any clashing attitudes.

But let us go back to Tolstoy. I think there is another interesting
parallel between Tolstoy and Athenagoras. The 'revolutionary' of Holy
Russia in many ways prepared the way for Lenin and Trotsky. Equally, the anti-dogmatist and liberal Athenagoras provided opportunities
for the Western world to demonstrate its solidarity with all Christian
denominations. But when the tragic events of 6 September 1955
occurred—the violent riots in Constantinople and Smyrna—he found
himself in a complete void. He was alone, without any support from the
liberals of Europe.

There is also a link between these two Orthodox personalities—
who lived in different periods in history—and another great personality
of the Far East, that great man of peace, Mahatma Gandhi. Gandhi, a
non-Christian, borrowed the early Christian ideal of non-resistance to
evil from Tolstoy, and he organized the campaign and worked out the
technique of passive resistance in India. Gandhi, in fact, used all the
bloodless weapons which Tolstoy recommended: opposition to capitalist
industry, encouragement of cottage industry, and the achievement of
personal and political freedom by restricting the dependence of India
on foreign interests. Hundreds of millions of people—the active revolu-

tionists of Russia and the passive revolutionists of India—adopted and
put into practice the ideas of Tolstoy, that reactionary revolutionary' of
nineteenth-century Russia.

The same applies to Athenagoras. When the Turkish mob set fire
to most of the Greek churches in Constantinople in September 1955,
he adopted the policy of passive resistance. All alone, he witnessed the
destruction and pillage of places of worship without a word of conso-
lation from the other Churches of Christ. He did not abandon his position—which is what his enemies hoped for—and he did not surrender
himself to the enraged mob to complete the tragedy by being hanged,
and so supply the Greek government of the time with a dramatic event
that would help to cover up their weaknesses. Instead of attacking the
Turkish government, he preferred to officiate quietly at services held
in small churches that had not been destroyed by the rioting mobs. He
also refrained from moving his seat of office to Moscow and thus sought
the intervention of the U.S.S.R. against Turkey. Instead, he adopted the
policy of passive resistance, hoping that this would provide an objective
lesson to the Turkish government and also to the Western and Eastern
worlds.

And yet one wonders whether the Patriarch's concept of a social,
moral, and religious system was understood by the materialistic world
in which we live any more, I would say, than the democracy of Plato or
the social contract of Jean Jacques Rousseau were understood by their
contemporaries.[39]

Athenagoras had no phobia of the machine, unlike Tolstoy, who
was terrified of the development of industry and the moral problems
that this would create. On the contrary, he thought that there was a
danger that the machine would provide an element of freedom at a
time when there was a lowering of morals, at a time when the nations

39. Ibid., p. 79.

and the churches were unable to sustain the spirit of love and cooperation. For this reason, he prophesied that atomic energy would either bring new freedom to mankind or cause its destruction. In fact, he believed in the second alternative. In his encyclical of Christmas 1976, he said:

There is another pessimistic point of view which forecasts a gloomy future for the world. According to this, the differences that divide Christians, the galloping progress of technology and especially of electronics, the pollution of the atmosphere and of the sea and rivers of the world, and of the environment as a whole are leading the world towards disaster.

ΩΩΩ

This is how he criticized with the pure conscience of the East 'the doctrine of death' of the West.

Now did all this mean that Athenagoras did not honor the spiritual tradition of Orthodoxy and that he was drawn more and more toward the Protestant world, as some of his enemies maintained? Quite the contrary. Athenagoras firmly believed in the spiritual tradition of Orthodoxy. To understand this tradition, however, we have to analyze the differences between Orthodox and Protestant traditions.

2. WESTERN AND ORTHODOX TRADITIONS

The Greek Orthodox and Protestant worlds are divided by a deep spiritual chasm, which to be understood has to be deeply analyzed.

According to Professor John Romanides, St Augustine teaches that the sin of Adam was inherited by all his descendants; so God condemned all humanity and passed a sentence of death. God, however, chose a group of people and 'predestined them for salvation.'

Those who were not chosen by God must not complain because as accomplices of Adam they must suffer their just punishment.

The Greek Fathers, on the other hand, have never accepted a moral, philosophical, or social system which is based on a so-called rigid metaphysical argument.

God was always the friend of all people; for this reason, the world was reconciled with God through Jesus Christ. Man becomes the enemy of God through sin and experiences the anger of God.

The Greek Fathers taught that God, not wanting death, nevertheless permitted death out of his love, so that evil and sin might not become eternal. Moreover, God recreated man through the Resurrection "by death trampling down death." God loves and perfects all men, but not all men are perfected to the same extent or degree.

Those who do not wish to relinquish an egotistical and self-indulgent life and to cooperate with God remain His enemies and do not merit His love. God created man so that he should live in peace, friendship, and solidarity with his fellow men.

Athenagoras, however, believed that this Orthodox tradition should be positive and should be renewed and readjusted to the realities and needs of a constantly changing society. The Church also had to renew its thinking and to adjust to contemporary issues. It was not a question of tactics or of policy; what he meant was that the Church was obliged to change its concepts because it came up against the dreadful realities of contemporary materialism. "The Church," he said "must not be a static institution. It must be the body of a living and dynamic Christ. Christian leaders must not stay dug in the trenches of yesterday; they must go over the top and become soldiers carrying the eternal message of God, which is love, unity, and work."

But how did he relate the duty of the Orthodox tradition to contemporary society? Athenagoras did not believe that with the remnants of virtues like charity our religious society could become again a lively force. With regret, he observed that Orthodox Greeks living in an industrial society became victims of the mania for wealth and material things. The religious ideals of peace, equality, and brotherhood were discarded and crushed by the sheer weight of the materialistic world. Everyone whose only ambition, whose only goal was to make money was a 'fine and respectable man.' The pure character of the Church had become tarnished by the powerful impact of a society that was insatiably greedy for financial gain and was always ready to make any concession, any sacrifice to achieve wealth and power.

He thought that pragmatism was the malignant growth of our times. It had set up the machine as a God and had turned men into hedonists, into automata without hearts, experts without souls.

He realized that if his fellowmen continued to think in this way, they would inevitably apply the same criteria to their relations with each other. Life had sunk to the level of things, of consumer goods; but if money gave a sort of social status, it failed to command the respect of a man with a soul and an intelligent mind. He, therefore, observed with sorrow and pain this mismarriage of the machine with the old patriarchal agricultural establishments of Orthodoxy, which were based on such values as love, self-respect, and dignity.

At this point, I must emphasize that Athenagoras drew inspiration from the moral values laid down by St Kosmas who, as you may remember, had lived in the Patriarch's own village approximately a century before Athenagoras was born. The Patriarch had great admiration for the teachings of St. Kosmas, and he always revered his memory.

3. ATHENAGORAS AND ST. KOSMAS

Often, when Athenagoras quoted from the teachings of Father Kosmas, he used the following excerpt:

And for this reason, my dear brothers, you must be glad if you earn your daily bread by your own efforts, because that kind of bread is blessed. Give some of this bread to the poor, because with it you can also buy paradise.

Similarly, those of you who live by perpetrating acts of injustice and plunder should shed black tears because God will descend upon you with wrath. If you are true Christian you should live by your sweat because God blesses such men and curses the unjust and the plunderers.

I have neither a sack for my belongings, nor a house, nor a clerical robe. The only thing I possess is a stool and I should be happy to give this to you. If I walked about looking for money, I would certainly be either stupid or a madman. I can live on a hundred grams of bread. God blesses this quantity of bread because it is necessary to sustain my body. But if I eat a hundred and ten drams of bread, the ten extra drams would be a waste. God would curse me because those extra ten drams belong to those that are hungry.

ΩΩΩ

Athenagoras shared Kosmas' dislike of luxury and ostentatiousness, because as Kosmas said: "There are poor people who have nothing. God did not give us wealth in order to over-eat, to wear expensive clothes, or to build tall palaces, while the poor people die of hunger."

Strangely enough, St. Kosmas was the cause of a difference of opinion I once had with the Patriarch. I remember it was in March 1950, when I was asked by the Greek Union Society of Istanbul to give a talk about St Kosmas Aitolos. The Patriarch read about my intended talk in the paper, and he was annoyed. "You must change the subject of your talk," he said to me. I understood what he was getting at; St Kosmas had been executed by the Turks during the Ottoman Empire, and he did not wish to stir up any ill feelings with the present-day Turks.

Looking rather sheepish, I replied, "I know what you mean, Your Holiness, but it's too late to cancel the talk. So I shall only talk about the teachings of Kosmas and make no reference to his death." Despite the fact that Athenagoras always forgave everyone, I think he felt a little hurt at my youthful daring and clumsiness for wanting to talk on such a tactless subject.

Anyway the next day after my talk he said to me: "Well, you managed to start quite a conflagration." But that's all he said.

Twenty years later, on the recommendation of Patriarch Athenagoras, the Holy Synod of the Ecumenical Patriarchate canonized Kosmas Aitolos as a saint. One day Athenagoras called me to his office, and without referring to the old incident he said to me: "I have a request to make. I would like you to go to my village Vassilikon to attend the dedication of the Church of St. Kosmas. I know how highly you think of him because St. Kosmas befriended the poor and the weak. I would like you to make the dedicatory address on my behalf." That was typical of Athenagoras!

4. THOUGHTS AND MEDITATION

Athenagoras studied life like a priest studies the Bible when he prepares to read a passage from the Gospel. Deep meditation is the complete withdrawal from the world of sensibility and the absolute concentration on a spiritual matter.

When he was Bishop of Corfu he used to say: "We suffer in life

because we turn it into a valley of tears, whereas God created it as
a garden of flowers. We think that the administrative and political
systems are to blame and we always forget that the Kingdom of God
is within us."

As the Ecumenical Patriarch, he used to confess:

I have no pleasures of my own. My pleasures are your pleasures.
Each day I talk with all of you, but each day I talk with each one of you
separately. I love dialogue. I consider it a blessing to receive people in
my office. I always remember those simple peasants in Monastir who
used to say to me 'we have just come to look at you.' There is philosophy for you I Every night when you are all asleep I walk down the aisle
of the church and I conduct another dialogue with Christ my Master
and Our Lady the Virgin Mary. I do it for the sake of all of you—here,
in America, in Australia, in Europe, everywhere...

ΩΩΩ

On one occasion in Corfu, journalists asked him to tell them something about his personal life. The Patriarch replied with a smile: "What
for? If I have been of help to some people, then this will be written in their
hearts. Write only this: 'There was a man named Athenagoras. Alone he
was nothing; just a grain of sand in the unlimited universe. The only thing
that made him worthwhile was that he devoted all his love to mankind.'"

His philosophy and the depth and sensitiveness of his thoughts are
well brought out in a long conversation he once had with Professor Olivier Clement, professor at the Institute of Orthodox Theology in Paris.
I would like to make one point about this conversation. When you read
Athenagoras' answers you must remember that he was speaking as the
leader of a very conservative and traditional Church, a Church which
had none of the liberal, open-minded attitudes of some of the Western
Churches. Therefore some of the ideas and concepts expressed in the
interview are, by the conservative standards of the Orthodox Church,

not only liberal but often quite revolutionary. With this reminder, I now quote excerpts from the interview with Professor Clement:

Patriarch Athenagoras: "Man suffers from constant anxiety. He cannot find himself. The more he conquers, the more his anxiety increases. He cannot find peace of mind. His heart yearns for the infinite, for a love without bounds. The repression of his desires for the infinite explains many of our contemporary upheavals."

Clement: "But how can we ignore the young intellectuals of the West, the spoilt children who have so much and who continuously acquire more and more. Yet they seem to possess nothing because they deny themselves a happiness, which they say, 'alienates' them from society."

Patriarch Athenagoras: "I think the young people are completely abandoned today. Their cry is the cry of an orphan; their distress is an appeal. And what do we do for them? We simply try to understand and to overcome the fear which seems to create the generation gap. We certainly talk a great deal, but we have no idea how to convert these grandiloquent words into action. I am afraid the younger generation have lost faith in us because they no longer believe in our speeches. They are demanding. Some people tell them that they must alter the world and change society that men will then be so content that they will forget all about God. This is not true; the more we satisfy the basic needs of man, the more the need for God becomes important This is because everyone dies."

Clement: "Often in your encyclicals at Christmas and Easter you mention that 'the Kingdom of God will come on Earth.'"

Patriarch Athenagoras: "We prepare the Kingdom of God on earth and earth will be transformed. I think that is the objective of all human values. Cultural civilization could predict and foreshadow the Kingdom of God."

Clement: "How is it possible to relate the great and tragic problems of mankind to the Resurrection?"

Patriarch Athenagoras: "One-third of mankind is starving, and to the hunger of the body we must add the hunger of the spirit. In fact, two-thirds of the world's population have never heard of the name of Jesus Christ. On the other hand, in countries, we call Christian there is a vast difference between the way of life as Christ saw it and the way of life as people live it. How can all of this be related to the Resurrection? But surely it is self-evident. The so-called Christians do not understand the meaning of the Resurrection and are unable to live up to its principles. They have lost touch with the spirit of the Gospel. They have converted Church into a machine, theology into a fictitious science, Christianity into a vague moral code. We must discover again the teachings of the Apostle Paul. If all those who believe in the Resurrection possess in themselves the vitality of life, they will be able to dispel the anxieties which today torture the minds of men."

Clement: "But men no longer know how to do this. The Church must help them to find Christ in themselves."

Patriarch Athenagoras: "I disagree. I think they understand much more than you suggest. The Bible is not the monopoly of Christians. Think for example of the work done by a man like Gandhi. It is true, of course, that the presence of Christ is partially concealed and that Church values have become detached from the essence of Christ, Who alone can give meaning to these values. At the same time, within the Church, a close cooperation must exist between the priests and the people because the people are the creatures of God. We, the men of the Church, can do nothing without the help of the ordinary people, because alone we, the men of the Church, run the risk of becoming isolated from life itself."

Clement: "In such a cooperation between the clergy and the people, what would you say should be the role of each side in an effort to solve all our great moral, social, and political problems?"

Patriarch Athenagoras: "I think the people must spontaneously assume their own responsibilities; they must not have them imposed on them, because that anyhow would be impossible. The work of the Church is to remind people of the real meaning of life and to help them become responsible human beings."

Clement: "In this context, what must we think of the Papal Encyclical Humanae Vitae about which there has been so much talk?"

Patriarch Athenagoras: "I know that the whole world has criticized it. But may I say this. The Pope had to talk in that way; he had no other alternative. You see in the Vatican there is a special language when dealing with this kind of problem. And the Pope used this kind of language, which I am sure is not entirely his own, because of tradition. We must understand that the Pope wished to defend certain values, for example, the sanctity of human love, the mystery of the child, and at the same time to attack the submission to dissipation and debauchery—where pleasure is unbridled and wanton, where there is no tenderness and no real love. The Pope also wished to defend the rights of the family against the new authoritarianism—the authoritarianism of technology which threatens it in certain countries of the neutral world."

Clement: "And what about us, the Orthodox?"

Patriarch Athenagoras: "Fortunately, we have no such great difficulty. But our clergy have much to say and to do. We must help the ordinary people become responsible individuals. We must certainly remind them of the real meaning of love. The love of a man and a woman is a wonderful aspect of Christian love because in this the love of Christ and of the Church is expressed. It is a great mystery which involves the gradual discovery of each other and of the infinity of life."

Clement: "Our Orthodox Church sanctifies married life. The ideal of human love is the bond created between one man and one woman. For this reason, our Church does not encourage a second marriage but only tolerates it. Yet the Church in its wisdom acknowledges that in certain cases a man and a woman do not come up to the expectations of the mystery of marriage. In such cases, it tolerates divorce and the marriage of divorced people. Nevertheless, divorce and a second marriage are not the rights of a Christian, but simply the extraordinary arrangements of an understanding society. To come up to the expectations of the mystery of marriage, one must devote one's whole life to it."

Patriarch Athenagoras: "The real attitude of the Church is not judicial but pastoral. The rules are curative indications and it is up to the bishop or the confessor to apply them to each particular case. But please note that in the Orthodox Church we have a rule which is not according to the Gospel. We ordain a married man, but we forbid an unmarried priest from marrying. This is not an ecclesiastical tradition; it is merely a custom which was enforced on the Church at a later date and which the Church is free to alter at any time."

Clement: "Yes, I do understand. But let us suppose that this custom is justified in certain traditional circles with this argument: 'human love can be extended to embrace the love that a priest must give to his own wife.' On the other hand, it is difficult to accept that an unmarried priest, who has already devoted his entire life to the Church, can divide his all-consuming love between the woman he marries and the Church."

Patriarch Athenagoras: "I do not understand this apportioning of love. If a woman marries a priest, she also loves him as a priest Therefore when she marries him she will help him in his work and help him do his duty to the Church. I believe that a priest should be allowed to marry after his ordination. It is unjust to oblige a man to search in haste and at random for a wife, simply so that he can get married before he becomes ordained. After all, men do not marry for the sake of getting married, but because they find a suitable person and because they fall in love. By the same token, a priest remains unmarried not because he wants to stay unmarried but simply because he has not found a suitable marriage partner. So I think a man should be allowed to marry when he finds such a person after his ordination. But in this regard, unfortu- nately, our Church is unjust. If we wish people to feel that Christianity means the Church, then the Church must be just in all matters."[40]

ΩΩΩ

5. DIALOGUE WITH CHRISTIAN CHURCHES

Athenagoras believed that Christians were divided; he believed that today, more than ever before, men need the teachings of the Gospel and that the ideal of cooperation between the Churches stands above the stupid and egotistical dogmatic differences that separated them. For Athenagoras, the twentieth century was the century of love and brotherhood and not the epoch of ecclesiastical jingoism. Earlier, self-satisfied Orthodoxy had isolated itself behind defensive walls and ramparts and refused to communicate and carry on a dialogue with the rest of the Christian world. If any efforts at communication had been made, these were simply superficial diplomatic disguises.

The tempestuous arrival of Athenagoras in Constantinople as Ecumenical Patriarch immediately started a strong policy reorien- tation. The new Patriarch, with twenty years experience of Western thought and culture, was unwilling to continue the stupid and useless war against the rest of the Christian world. He firmly believed in a pan-Christian dialogue, and he guided the Orthodox Church towards a more liberal path, including cooperation with the World Council of

40. O. Clement, Dialogues avec le patriarche Athenagoras (Paris, 1969), pp. 127-28, 139,14243, 144,165-66, 169-71.

Churches, so that he could communicate with the Eastern Churches, but also in order to balance by means of the presence of the Orthodox Church the pan-Protestant movement against Catholicism. In this way, the ramparts of the Orthodox Church were demolished and the parochial concept of the 'superiority' of the Orthodox Church was gradually obliterated. So without hysterical outbursts from within 'the stronghold,' Orthodoxy, strong in the belief in itself, came out into the open to discuss and communicate the truth with other denominations. Therefore, the greatest victory of the Orthodox Church was that which was achieved against its own obsessive traditionalism and its deep-rooted rigidity.

6. YOUTH

Athenagoras saw clearly that the totally unjustified Second World War had deeply scarred the values of the civilized world. Only ashes remained in the hearts of men and especially in the hearts of the younger men and women. "Meantime," he said in his encyclical of Christmas 1970, "the youth of the world expresses its militancy either by passive resistance or with violent incidents demanding the change of all leadership and the destruction of every accepted social order. Youth continues to search for a new world and wants to create a new order."

Therefore the relations of the younger generation with the Christian Churches—which had been unable to prevent the Second World War—took on a new character. Relegated to the very edge of modern history—which was tantamount to spiritual sterility—the Christian Churches were incapable of promoting the ideals of love and solidarity and were thus unable to inject any vitality into the concept of peace among nations. From that moment on, the Christian Churches were deprived of their impact and lost the support of the younger generation.

Therefore it was natural for Athenagoras to believe that the younger generation would seek methods to oppose the status quo, which they thought was too conservative and reactionary. Athenagoras believed that the younger generation was well-intentioned by moral aspirations which the contemporary post-war establishment had been unable to put into practice so as to give youth some kind of leadership. He did not blame the young, who had to face some pretty difficult problems in a post-war society which was too conformist intellectually, socially, and politically. He certainly thought that there was a great deal to be said in favor of the young people. However, he also realized that the young themselves, while revolting against an amoral established society, had no moral or social policy to put into practice simply because they too were victims of the conditions against which they revolted.

7. INTELLECTUAL COMMUNICATION

Although the Western Christian Churches were unable to prevent the Second World War, Athenagoras realized that there was a great deal of strength and positiveness in these Churches. He accepted that the Protestant and Catholic Churches had created, through an interchange of ideas, a common attitude toward the great problems of philosophy, communication, and politics. On the other hand, the Orthodox Church itself was far removed from any such enlightened social developments. He was of the opinion that as Christians belonging to the Eastern Orthodox Church, modern Greeks did not conform in private life to the moral and other standards which were inherent in their religion. In other words, outside the Church, the daily life of the Orthodox Greeks seemed to bear little relation to his religious code.

He observed with regret that the ruling class tended towards nepotism and favoritism and that this state of things had created a confused morality; people looked upon the criticisms of yesterday with a great deal of cynicism because they knew that tomorrow the same criticism would be turned into praise. With the present ruling class, it was impossible to eradicate poverty, to uproot oppression and human cruelty, and to stop theft in the big cities. The younger generation lacked the good example of a truly Orthodox life.

Spiritual community exists in a society where the majority of the educated people share a positive intellectual interest of which they are proud. For example, in the Germany between the two wars, men of various professions, like lawyers, doctors, scientists, industrialists, and others had a common intellectual bond in communicating with each other because when the first man started quoting from Goethe, the second man took up the quotation, and then the third man finished it off. Despite their different educational backgrounds, the common and positive intellectual link was Goethe. They were not isolated in their own particular professions because they were inspired by a common intellectual heritage which enabled them to converse and exchange points of view. So we see that intellectual society is made up of people who share common intellectual and moral values. Goethe, Stefan George, or Rilke in Germany, or Racine in France, formed the foundation of these intellectual communications. There was another important factor, namely, that all these countries possessed a recent literary past, and this helped a great deal.[41]

In contrast Greece had no recent intellectual past. The only intellectual movement which could deal with the international philosophical, political, and literary problems of the day was that of Constantinople; but the Phanariot culture, despite the ability of its ecclesiastical members, was rather repressive of the ideas that infiltrated

41. P. Kanel lopoulos, "He pneumatike neoellenike koinonia," Megale Hellenike Egkyklopaideia Pyrsou I, 860.

from Europe into liberated Greece. In fact, it was a society which was acutely rigid and conventional and which tended to promote sterile ideas and to act as a damper on the development of the neo-Hellenic culture.

8. GREEK NEO-FATHERHOOD

Athenagoras had a deep appreciation of the Christian philosophy of life. He was an anti-aristocrat, a proletarian, a lover of the poor, the meek, and all those scorned by society. He truly believed in the biblical passage "Blessed are the meek, for they shall inherit the earth."

In the protocol of Athenagoras there were no superiors or inferiors, but only the messengers of love—all equal in duty and responsibility toward their fellowmen.

Athenagoras admired more than anything else the Sermon on the Mount The superiority of the human mind, wisdom, knowledge, science, and even ethics are of no value when compared with the simple, warm heart of an ordinary man who understands nothing of the achievements of the intellect and who cannot with his knowledge and set habits of character differentiate between the correct and the incorrect. For love to exist, there must be life. Man was created so that love can triumph, and yet at every turn, Athenagoras saw the triumph of injustice. But he controlled his bitterness at the injustice that the strong and mighty could inflict on all those who through circumstances were unable to put an end to their suffering and sacrifices. Of course, sacrifice comes naturally to one who loves. He accepted that the strong of the earth are inhuman violators; their ego, an unassailable citadel; their philosophy, the derision of those who are weak. But he could not hate them because he was a Christian, and as he had devoted his life to love he could not suddenly put on the cloak of hate.

He had gone beyond the first phase in the struggle for individu-
alism; he had rejected the ferocious face of the fighter. He believed in
a society which was built on the principle of respect for the individual,
for Christians of all denominations, for all men on earth. To use an
unusual simile, one could say that a charismatic man is a sort of earth-
quake which in fact creates and reshapes history itself. Athenagoras was
certainly such a man because, with his intellect his tremendous magnet-
ic personality, and his drive, he reshaped the intellectual and spiritual
destiny of the Orthodox Church.

ΩΩΩ

CHAPTER 5

CONCLUSION

Athenagoras, by the mercy of God Archbishop of Constantinople, New Rome, and Ecumenical Patriarch, died in July 1972 aged eighty-six, at the Orthodox Hospital of Baloukli, Istanbul. He died a few days after he fell down some stairs in the Patriarchal Residence.

His funeral was held in the Church of St. George at the Patriarchate and was attended by high dignitaries of the Christian Churches—including the then Archbishop of Canterbury, Dr. Michael Ramsay, the Archbishop of Athens, Hieronymos, and by the entire Greek community of Istanbul, as well as Greeks from other towns in Turkey. He was buried at the cemetery of Baloukli next to the tombs of all the other Ecumenical Patriarchs who died since the fall of Constantinople in 1453.

Athenagoras died as he lived, a poor man; throughout his life, all his financial resources went to the poor and destitute. At the time of his death, his entire fortune consisted of a few Turkish pounds, which were found in a chest next to a divan that he used as a bed. The exalted Patriarch lived in two modest rooms: one, which he used as a drawing room-office, and the other, an even smaller rather dingy room, which he used as his bedroom. The example of the frugal life led by St. Kosmas Aitolos was always uppermost in the Patriarch's mind.

Of course, the death of Athenagoras was mourned throughout the world. But the important thing was not the mourning according to protocol, the formal mourning of the officials and dignitaries, but the sincere tears of the ordinary people. It was the mourning of the masses for the loss of one of their great spiritual leaders, a man who personified the triumph of the spirit over the material world. Now he was dead. Now both the Orthodox Church and the Greek nation were fatherless. And so they wept the genuine tears of an orphan.

If you did not know Athenagoras and you met him for the first time, you immediately asked: "Who is he? Who is that man who seems to radiate sunshine?"—because you could almost feel the strength of his love issuing forth from his eyes, from his face, from his hands, from his whole body. There was no room in that body for hate. Other men became famous because of material power, because they had won battles, made territorial conquests, or because they had built up business or technological empires.

What was the material power of Athenagoras? Well, I think you might say that it consisted of his humble steward at the Patriarchal Residence, who had served him faithfully during the twenty or more years that he was Ecumenical Patriarch!

For sixty-five years Athenagoras was at the ramparts of the Church and of the Greek nation. His journey through these sixty-five years was triumphant. Corfu never forgot him because of the great services he rendered to the island and its inhabitants. The emigrants of

the United States—where he united a wholly dissident Greek community—swore by his name. From New York, he went to Istanbul where
he remained for twenty years—Istanbul, the place that became his own
Golgotha.

On 6 September 1955, "the curtain of the Temple was torn in
two from top to bottom." The Greeks of Constantinople walked in
streets strewn with broken glass to their homes, which were without
doors or windows, and to their shops, which had been smashed and
ransacked. There was little that was not plundered. It was a world of
despair. Churches in ruins. Priests that had fled. Who had the courage
to stay in that holocaust? Because of Makarios, the rioters were ready to
take revenge on his brother in Christ, the Patriarch. It was an opportunity for sacrifice for Athenagoras. A Patriarch clasping a cross to his
bosom and a staff in his hand could go out into the streets and meet his
death at the hands of the incensed crowds. One more martyr for the
Greek Church? Athenagoras thought about it. Yes, it would be good
to have another martyr's halo, another hero's statue. Yes, but it would
also mean the creation of another symbol of hate to divide the Greek
and Turkish people for a few more centuries! Would that serve the real
purpose of the Church and of the Ecumenical Throne? No, because if
the person of the Patriarch disappeared from the Phanar there would
be new developments, there would be other successors! And who would
be his successor? Where would he come from? No, it would have been a
useless and harmful sacrifice.

Moreover, the Patriarchate was surrounded by the Turkish army,
and entry or exit from it was forbidden while the riots continued.
Should the Patriarch disobey the orders? What a wonderful scene that
would be—the leader of the Orthodox Church having a fistfight with
the sergeant of the guard, and the sergeant pulling and pushing the
Patriarch to prevent him from breaking the regulations. So there were

only two alternatives: either an action of heroism, to be slaughtered by
the extremists, or an action of diplomatic expediency, which predictably
meant inactivity, staying inside the isolated Patriarchal Residence and
doing nothing. The Patriarch had to choose the second alternative, dictated by incisive logic. Threats would have been dangerous. The search
for "protectors" outside the frontiers of Turkey, useless. At any rate,
such an appeal for foreign help would have had disastrous results for
the Ecumenical Patriarchate and unfavorable consequences for Western
policy.[42]

"Your Holiness, do you still believe in a Graeco-Turkish rapprochement?" asked Paul Paleologos, a close friend of the Patriarch.

Athenagoras, who usually replied without hesitation, paused for
a moment, looked at his friend, and then said two words, "I do." It was
difficult for him to say that "I do"; but the had to say it. If he wanted to
put up an opposition he had all the means at his disposal, both ecclesiastical and political. All he had to do was to move his little finger and
help would immediately be forthcoming. But at what a price! So, he
preferred to curb any impatient impulses and to listen to the voice of
cold logic, which spoke for the good of the majority.

He remembered that on another occasion he had been given the
opportunity for heroism. This was when he was called as a witness at
the trial of Adnan Menderes in 1956. He was the second Patriarch after
Gregory V—hanged by the Turks in 1821—who was brought to Turkish justice. At the time, he could have resigned and gained the respect
of all the Orthodox world. This would have been easy for him to do.
But then he thought about the Patriarchate, which exists in Istanbul by
custom; he thought of the Greek communities in Turkey; he thought of

42. P. Palaiologos, Hoi Hellenes exo apo ten Hellada; Orthodoxia kai
genos (Athens, 1972), p.29.

the delicate subject of Graeco-Turkish cooperation. And what in fact would have been the consequences of his opposition? A great power called the U.S.S.R.—who although denying the existence of God, used the Church for political purposes—was ready to don the mantle of protection of Orthodoxy and gradually take over the Patriarchal Throne at the Phanar. In fact, it seems that the Kremlin had suggested to Athenagoras that it would consider him as a de facto Patriarch who simply took refuge in Moscow following the persecution of his Church by the Turks. But Athenagoras disliked playing politics. He preferred to remain at his See and incur the criticism of 'his friends' and avoid the exploitation of 'his enemies,' in the hope that one day the judgment of the Christian world would finally justify his actions.

But let us once more cast a glance at the great work Athenagoras did for Christianity. He was a leader who created history: he revoked the ex-communications of 1054 which for eleven centuries divided the Orthodox and Catholic Churches without good reason. He offered instead the communion of love without limitations, a whole-hearted love that would solve all problems and abolish all differences.

It was the same love that made Pope Paul visit the Cathedral of Haghia Sophia while he was the guest of the Patriarch in Istanbul. The Pope, instead of being a visitor to a museum, became a pilgrim to a holy place. It is recorded that Pope Paul said to the Turkish foreign minister, who accompanied him on this historic visit: "With your permission, Your Excellency, I wish to pray in this holy place because before it became a museum, it was the House of God."

Equally moving were the parting words which Athenagoras uttered when he said goodbye to the Pope after his visit to the Vatican in 1965. "I am an old man. I do not know whether we shall meet again on earth. But be sure that in Heaven we shall enjoy together the blessing of seeing our two Churches united again. I say this because I know

that I personally shall not live long enough to see it happen on earth."
The union of the two Churches was of course not accomplished. But
Athenagoras was happy to see that progress was being made.

Another memorable event in his life was his meeting with Pope
Paul in Jerusalem in December 1964. This really was a revolutionary
act against ecclesiastical protocol. However, Athenagoras had sought
something more radical to which, unfortunately, the Pope did not agree.
Athenagoras wanted a sort of round table conference over Christ's
tomb of all the leaders of the Christian Churches. He wanted this because he always tried to be a sort of bridge between the Protestant and
Catholic world.

I suppose the most difficult and uncomfortable part of his life—
not that there was much material comfort in Athenagoras' life—was
that which he spent at the Phanar, this neglected quarter of the city
of Istanbul which is damp, dirty, and noisy. All around the Patriarchal
Residence are minarets, and the dingy, narrow streets are filled with
busy shops, bazaars, and rowdy coffee houses. All day long and late into
the night the radios blare out Turkish music and songs and the hubbub
is such that you feel you are more in a marketplace than in the center of
sacred Eastern Christendom.

That is where Athenagoras spent twenty years of his life. His only
weapon was the Cross of Love; his lips were always whispering, always
speaking, always. crying out so that the whole Christian world would
hear his message of Christian love, peace, and concord. Many heard
this message and understood it; others pretended not to hear; still, others turned the other way. But it made no, difference to Athenagoras. He
knew his mission and he was determined, whatever the price, to sow the
seed of, universal love.

The great archpriest of Orthodoxy went to Istanbul in order to
fashion the arid inheritance of the Orthodox Christian and transform it

into a vital tradition. Ordinary inheritance is simply to repeat mechanically all those things said by your ancestors. Real tradition means that you take the best of the old social and moral institutions and alter them and adjust them to contemporary conditions and realities, thereby imbuing them with a new lease on life. Athenagoras gave Orthodoxy a new, dynamic lease on life. He secured for it the high position it deserves among the religions of the world.

And yet one thought saddens me: the thought that the enormous crowd which went to meet the Patriarch on his arrival at the airport in Istanbul on 26 January 1949 never realized what kind of a man they were meeting. They never realized that the tall, black-robed, white-bearded giant who stepped off a modern jet aircraft to meet them was indeed a man sent by God!

ΩΩΩ

End NOTES

Foreword

1. Informations Catholiques Internationales, No. 320 (Jan. 15, 1969).

2. A. G. Panotis, Paulos vi. Athenagoras A Eirenopoioi (Athens, 1971), pp: 43-44.

3. D. Tsakonas, " Athenagoras A'," Threskeutike kai Christianike Egkyklopaideia I, 602-06.

4. Ibid.

5. Panotis, p. 44.

6. J. Theodorakopoulos, "Ho Oikoumenikos Patriarches Athenagoras ho A', Paneuropi-Hellenismos 15 (Sept. 1973), 13.

Chapter 1

1. I. Panagopoulos, "Ho Patriarches Athenagoras Ho Megalos tes Orthodoxias," Christianos 131-37 (1972), 66.

2. Olivier Clement, "Ho Athenagoras aphegeitai," To Vema (Feb. 9, 1972).

3. Ibid.

4. Ibid.

5. Panagopoulos, p. 66.

6. An ecclesiastical group that refused to accept the Gregorian Calendar and continued to follow the Julian Calendar, which is thirteen days behind the Gregorian Calendar.

7. V. Stavrides, "Ho Oikoumenikos Patriarches Athenagoras ho A'," Stachys (1972), 308.

8. Panotis, p. 46.

9. Ibid.

10. I. D. Skiadopoulos,"Apo ta pepragmena mias oktaetias," Apolytrosis 72-76 (1973), 18.

11. Ibid., pp. 25-26.

12. Ibid.

13. Ibid., pp. 11, 17.

14. K. Bones, "Athenagoras ho A' ho Oikoumenikos Patriarches," Ekklesia 49 (1972), 397.

Chapter 2

1. Panotis, p. 39Z.

2. Archbishop Hieronymos, "Athenagoras ho A', "Ekklesia 49 (1972), 394.

3. Panotis, p. 39Z.

4. Bones, p. 402.

5. Matthew 19:20

6. 1 Corinthians 13"1-3

7. Archbishop Athenagoras of Thyateira, p. 436.

Chapter 3

1. Stavrides, p.312.

2. In Panotis, p. 57.

3. K. Sfyris, Hypo poles pro ypotheseis he Hellas einai yiosimos? (Athens, 1931), p.67.

4. That is, the re-establishment of the Byzantine Empire with Constantinople as its capital.

5. G. Theotokas, Pneumatikeporeia (Athens, N.D.), p.48.

6. See U. Rahner, Vom Ersten bis zum Outten Rom (Innsbruck, 1949), p. 18.

7. Panotis, pp. 41-42.

8. Ibid., p.-92.

9. Metropolitan Chrysostomos of Myra, "He arsis tou anathema-tos," Poimen (1973), 69.

10. Panotis, p. 183.

Chapter 4

1. Stefan Zweig, Ho kosmos tes Technes (Athens, N D.), p.64.

2. Ibid., p.65.

3. Ibid., pp. 65-67.

4. Ibid., p.70.

5. Ibid., p. 72.6. Panotis, p. 45.

7. Zweig, p. 75.

8. Ibid., p. 79.

9. O. Clement, Dialogues avec le patriarche Athenagoras (Paris, 1969), pp. 127-28, 139,14243, 144,165-66, 169-71.

10. P. Kanel lopoulos, "He pneumatike neoellenike koinonia," Megale Hellenike Egkyklopaideia Pyrsou I, 860.

Chapter 5

1. P. Palaiologos, Hoi Hellenes exo apo ten Hellada: Orthodoxia kai genos (Athens, 1972), p.29.

INDEX OF NAMES

Turks, 7, 8, 9, 32, 55, 74, 88

U

United States, 3, 24, 26, 30, 61,66

Umberto, Cardinal, 61

U.S.S.R., 49, 69, 88

government of, 60

V

Vassilikon, 7, 8, 11, 74

Vatican, 53, 55,60, 61, 62, 64, 78, 89

First Council of, 54

Second Council of, 53, 54, 55, 59,60

Venizelist, 25

Venizelos, Eleftherios, 39

Vezanis, 49

Villain, Maurice, 1

Virgin Mary, 75

Vitol i. 66

Voulgaris, family of, 22

W

Wallachia, 33

Washington, 46

Western Church, 13

Willbrans, Cardinal, 68

World War II, 45-46

Y

Yannina, 8

Ypsilantis, Alexander, 33

www.ingramcontent.com/pod-product-compliance
Lightning Source LLC
LaVergne TN
LVHW091224080426
835509LV00009B/1153